Basic Tools of RESEARCH

An Annotated Guide for Students of English

PHILIP H. VITALE

Professor of English, De Paul University

BARRON'S EDUCATIONAL SERIES, INC.
GREAT NECK, NEW YORK

All inquiries should be addressed to
BARRON'S EDUCATIONAL SERIES, INC.
343 GREAT NECK ROAD
GREAT NECK, NEW YORK

Printed in the United States of America

Library of Congress Catalog Card No. 62-17626

PREFACE

BASIC TOOLS OF RESEARCH is a highly selective list intended to serve the needs of undergraduate and graduate English majors as a handy work of reference or as a text for courses in bibliography and research. It differs from similar bibliographic manuals principally in: (1) its arrangement, which is designed to answer the requirements, not of the scholar or professional investigator, but of the student who lacks general conversance with the basic works of reference in his field or with the proper procedure to be followed in referring to them; and (2) its emphasis upon annotation.

Although the number of items brought together in this manual is relatively small, the experience of sixteen years of college teaching has convinced me that the typical undergraduate English major—the same holds generally true of the graduate English major—has a merely nominal or titular knowledge of no more than one hundred of the two hundred and eighty five basic tools of research contained in this work, and a practical or working knowledge of perhaps less than fifty.

Much is made currently of the glaring inadequacies of our students in linguistic expression, of the crucial need to deepen and to expand the thresholds of knowledge, and of the difficult task faced by colleges and universities as they seek to correct these inadequacies. Comparatively little is said of the correlative weakness of students in bibliography. But to know where and how to gain access to certain facts and ideas is a form of knowledge in itself, as well as a knowledge which is indispensable to the acquisition of the facts and ideas themselves. Lacking a proper awareness of the essential tools of research, the searcher of fact or truth either fails completely to gain his end, or he gains it at an expenditure of time and energy quite incommensurate to the end.

BASIC TOOLS OF RESEARCH is the result of a belief that a greater service may be rendered the student by exposing him to a brief list of some 285 items, which he can be expected to master, and which will meet most, if not all, of his needs, than to expose him to a work, say, of 2,000 items or more, which he finds overwhelming and often confusing, and which probably contains hundreds of works which he will never have occasion to consult.

A glance at the Table of Contents will reveal the principle of arrangement: from the most general to the most specific; from the earliest to the most current. When an item (usually a learned journal or a bibliography of dissertations) is listed a second time, the student is referred to the first listing for the annotation. Brief excerpts from reviews in most instances follow the formal annotation of the work.

Handbooks, bibliographies, and concordances of individual major writers and works are generally omitted. The representative English major can be expected to know of their existence and can usually gain ready access to them.

Table of Contents

GUIDES

MINTO, John.
Reference Books: A Classified and Annotated Guide to the Principal Works of Reference. London: Library Association, 1929–1931. 2 vols., 356 p. and 140 p.

The "British Mudge"; standard for English students.

MUDGE, Isadore.
A Guide to Reference Books. 6th ed. Chicago: American Library Association, 1936.

Appreciably fuller than the fifth edition and containing a valuable addition of business reference works. In many instances, however, the supplementary references remain dated.

MURPHEY, Robert W.
How and Where to Look it Up. New York: McGraw-Hill Book Company, Inc., 1958. 721 p.

Intended "to fill the needs of . . . occasional or frequent users of reference sources to whom the intricacies of library science are largely a mystery."

ROBERTS, Arthur D.
Introduction to Reference Books. London: Library Association, 1956. 237 p.

Intended as a text for students taking the course in librarianship at the University College, London. Describes various kinds of reference books, cites some titles as examples, but does not attempt to list works in special subject fields. Useful, but from the British point of view.

SHORES, Louis.
Basic Reference Books: A General Introduction to the Evaluation, Study, and Use of Reference Materials. Chicago: American Library Association, 1939. 472 p.

Basic Reference Sources: An Introduction to Materials and Methods. With a Chapter on Science Reference Sources by Helen Focke. Chicago: American Library Association, 19–54. 378 p.

Based upon BASIC REFERENCE BOOKS (2nd ed. 1939 o.p.). Describes 147 types of source essentials; gives 554 basic reference titles. Titles of works published after Dec. 1951 are not included.

WINCHELL, CONSTANCE M.
Guide to Reference Books. Chicago: American Library Association, 7th ed., 1951. 645 p. First Supplement, 1954; Second Supplement, 1956; Third Supplement, 1960.

Based upon GUIDE TO REFERENCE BOOKS, 6th ed., by Isadore Mudge. Describes over 5,500 titles in various languages, arranged by subjects. The First Supplement to the Seventh Edition lists approximately 1,000 reference works published generally from 1950 through 1952. The Second Supplement to the Seventh Edition lists almost 1,200 reference works published generally from 1953 through 1955. The Third Supplement to the Seventh Edition lists approximately 1,230 works published for the most part from 1956 through 1958. The selection of titles in the supplements follows the same general principles used in the main volume.

DICTIONARIES

Unabridged

Century Dictionary and Cyclopedia: With a New Atlas of the World. New York: Century Company, 1911. 12 vols.

A very comprehensive, encyclopedic type of dictionary; too old for general and current use, but still valuable for its careful treatment of scientific and technical terms, especially those that have significantly altered in meaning, and for its excellent illustrations and plates. Volumes one to ten constitute the dictionary proper; volume eleven comprises a cyclopedia of names,—biographical, geographical, fictitious, mythological; volume twelve is an atlas.

A Dictionary of American English on Historical Principles. Chicago: University of Chicago Press, 1936–1944. 4 vols.

Aims to evidence those elements by which American English is distinguished from the English spoken elsewhere, and thus includes "not only words or phrases which are clearly or apparently of American origin, or have greater currency here than elsewhere, but also every word denoting something which has a real connection with the development of the country and the history of its people."—Cf. "Preface," p. v. A definitive study of American English and thus indispensable, but of limited value to the student of twentieth-century American English, since it does not generally include matter extending beyond the end of the nineteenth century.

Funk and Wagnalls New Standard Dictionary of the English Language. New York: Funk and Wagnalls, 1947. 2814 p.

A well-edited dictionary including within the same alphabet more than 450,000 words, as well as some 65,000 proper names, and about 30,000 geographical names. The "Appendix" contains a list of foreign words and phrases, disputed pronunciations, rules for simplified spelling, and population statistics.

New Century Dictionary of the English Language. New York: Appleton-Century, 1948. 2 vols., 2798 p.

Not an abridgement of the CENTURY DICTIONARY AND CYCLOPEDIA as such. Although the vocabulary is selected from the CENTURY, the definitions are revised and the illustrative quotations are different. Includes more than 100,000 entries and more than 12,000 illustrative quotations.

New English Dictionary on Historical Principles. Oxford: Clarendon Press, 1888–1933. 10 vols. and supplement. Reissued, 1933 in 13 vols. under the title OXFORD ENGLISH DICTIONARY.

Its main purpose is to trace the history of every word included from the date of its introduction into the language, and illustrating changes of meaning, spelling, pronunciation, and usage by quotations from the writings of more than 5000 authors of all periods. "The complete work has a total vocabulary of 414,-825 words and includes 1,827,306 quotations."

"To students of language the O.E.D. is a sort of recurring marvel which never ceases its glamour," but only those who use it intensively can "know how it improves volume by volume in scope, thoroughness, and elaboration of detail."—(Ernest Weekley in the ATLANTIC MONTHLY)

Webster's Third New International Dictionary of the English Language, Unabridged. Editor-in-chief, Philip Babcock Gove. Springfield, Massachusetts: G. & C. Merriam Co. 2662 p.

Unlike its predecessors, the latest edition has been edited from the viewpoint of descriptive linguistics. Current usages and pronunciations are recorded, but the preferred form is not clearly indicated. Many of the pronunciation symbols of the earlier edition are retained, a few substitutions are made, and some have been dropped completely. According to the editors, 100,000 new words and definitions, using illustrative quotations from contemporary sources, have been added; but most of the new words and definitions, it must be noted, are in the area of scientific and technological reference. Instead of full treatment of a group of related terms, each term is defined at its own alphabetical place, and definition by synonym is carefully avoided. Among the special features, to follow the Preface, are: "(1) the recognition and separate entry (with part-of-speech label) of verb-plus-adverb compounds (as RUN DOWN) that function like one word verbs in every way except for having a separable suffix . . . (3) the recognition (by using the label OFTEN ATTRIB) of nouns that often function as adjectives but otherwise do not behave like the class of adjectives . . . (6) the recognition (by not using at all the status label COLLOQUIAL) that it is impossible to know whether a word out of context is colloquial or not, and (7) the incorporation of abbreviations alphabetically in the main vocabulary."

"The editors of the Third Edition have made a conscientious and usually successful attempt to determine the meanings and statuses of words by examination of their use in contexts and not by applying irrelevant historical, logical, or etymological criteria" —(HARPER'S, February, 1962).

"Instead, we have seen a century and a third of illustrious history largely jettisoned; we have seen a novel dictionary formula improvised, in great part out of snap judgments and the sort of theoretical improvement that in practice impairs; and we have seen the gates propped wide open in enthusiastic hospitality to miscellaneous confusions and corruptions. In fine, the anxiously awaited work that was to have crowned cisatlantic linguistic scholarship with a particular glory turns out to be a scandal and a disaster. Worse yet, it plumes itself on its faults and parades assiduously cultivated sins as virtues without precedent . . . We get dictionaries expressly that they may settle such problems for us. This dictionary seems to make a virtue of leaving them in flux, with the explanation that many matters are subjective and that the individual must decide for himself—a curious abrogation of authority in a work extolled as 'more useful and authoritative than any previous dictionary' "—(Wilson Follett, "Sabotage in Springfield," THE ATLANTIC, January, 1962).

"Most libraries will need both the 2d and 3d editions"—(LIBRARY JOURNAL, April 15, 1962).

Abridged Dictionaries

American College Dictionary, ed. by Clarence L. Barnhart, with the assistance of 355 authorities and specialists. New York: Random House, 1947. 1432 p.

Designed especially for use in schools, offices, and homes, and contains, in one alphabet about 120,000 entries, including proper names of persons and places, foreign words and phrases, abbreviations, etc. The current meanings are given first, the order for each entry being determined by the principle of frequency.

Webster's New Collegiate Dictionary. 6th ed. Springfield, Mass.: Merriam, 1956. 1196 p.

An entirely new work, not merely a revision; abridged directly from the second edition of the NEW INTERNATIONAL. Includes more than 126,000 entries, the new additions being principally in the scientific and technical fields and in the appendixes: abbreviations; arbitrary signs and symbols; over 5000 biographical names, with pronunciations, dates, and identifying phrases; some 10,000 names of places, colleges and universities in the United States and Canada; vocabulary of rhymes; orthography; punctuation.

Webster's New World Dictionary of the American Language, College Edition. Ed. by Joseph H. Friend and David B. Guralnik. Cleveland: The World Publishing Company, 1953, 1955. 1724 p.

Differs from the two-volumed "encyclopedic edition," which has 2068 pages, in that the latter has more appendixes. The 142,000 words, arranged in a single alphabet, includes vocabulary; biographical, geographical, Biblical, and classical names; foreign words and phrases; abbreviations; and a relatively extensive list of synonyms and antonyms. The emphasis is on current American usage.

The Concise Oxford Dictionary of Current English. Adapted from the original by H. W. and F. G. Fowler; 4th ed. rev. by E. McIntosh. New York: Oxford University Press, 1951. 1524 p.

Concerned principally with British words which are in current use or found frequently in quotations or proverbs; technical terms which are generally current, not purely erudite; and colloquialisms, slang, and vulgar expressions. Based upon the OXFORD ENGLISH DICTIONARY, but not an abridgement of it as such. Often cited as the C.O.D.

The Shorter Oxford English Dictionary. Ed. by William Little, H. W. Fowler and J. Coulson, revised and edited by C. T. Onions. New York: Oxford University Press, 1957. 2 vols.

An abridgement of THE OXFORD ENGLISH DICTIONARY, achieved principally by the omission of quotations and the extensive use of abbreviations. Includes "all words in regular literary and colloquial use" and a selected list of technical, archaic, and scientific words.

Although not a complete substitute for the O.E.D., it is "nevertheless an invaluable introduction to and aid in the use of the larger work" – (SATURDAY REVIEW OF LITERATURE).

More revealing of the life of words "than any other dictionary of comparable size" – (NATION, 1933).

Funk and Wagnalls Standard Dictionary of the English Language. International ed. New York: Funk and Wagnalls, 1958. 1506 p.

An intermediate size standard dictionary. Attempts to include "the established word stock of English and of the rapidly expanding vocabularies of the arts, sciences, trades, and professions," slang, colloquialisms, and regional and local dialects. Arranges in a single letter by letter alphabet: personal, proper, and geographical names, foreign phrases, etc. Following the main text are arranged some 5,000 commonly used abbreviations.

Funk and Wagnalls New College Standard Dictionary of the English Language. Emphatype Edition. Ed. by Charles Earle Funk. New York: Funk and Wagnalls, 1947. 1404 p.

Based on the NEW STANDARD DICTIONARY OF THE ENGLISH LANGUAGE. The largest of the abridged "standard" dictionaries, it features a new system of pronunciation, following which stressed syllables are underscored. Emphasis is on current usage. Etymologies follow the definitions.

A Dictionary of Americanisms on Historical Principles. Ed. by Mitford McLeod Mathews. Chicago: University of Chicago Press, 1951. 2 vols., 1946 p.

Narrower in scope than A DICTIONARY OF AMERICAN ENGLISH ON HISTORICAL PRINCIPLES, embracing fewer words, but including those of more modern appearance and giving further emphasis to slang and dialect. Illustrated with some 400 line drawings.

"It is virtually a source book, continental in its range and diversity, of American experience in its most completely American aspects" – (NEW YORK HERALD TRIBUNE, 1951).

WORDBOOKS

ADAMS, Ramon F.
Western Words: A Dictionary of the Range, Cow Camp and Trail. Norman: University of Oklahoma Press, 1944. 182 p.

A readable and invaluable collection of some 3,000 words and phrases of cowboy lingo, alphabetically arranged and providing etymologies of derivative words.

A delightful collection of words and phrases dealing "with the cattle business" and containing "extended discussions of the origins of such terms as 'maverick,' 'dogie,' etc."—(NEW YORKER)

A work "that will edify scholars and philologists and delight lay readers"—(BOOK WEEK, December 24, 1944).

ALLEN, Edward F.
A Dictionary of Abbreviations and Symbols. London: Cassell and Company, 1949. 224 p.

A collection of over 6,000 abbreviations and symbols usually encountered in literature, art, education, politics, religion, industry, war, and especially, business; but weak in the field of mathematics, specialized science, and foreign abbreviations. Includes more symbols than most of the better known dictionaries of abbreviations and symbols.

BERREY, L. V. and M. Van Den Bark.
The American Thesaurus of Slang: A Complete Reference Book of Colloquial Speech. 2d ed. New York: Thomas Y. Crowell & Company, 1953. 1280 p.

Over 10,000 expressions arranged in parts, general slang and colloquialisms, and subdivided into categories determined by dominant ideas, occupations, etc.; contains an alphabetical word index for easy reference.

Presents "a vivid introduction to the past and present vitality of the American language. The synonyms and antonyms cover the broad subject of life from natural phenomena through social organization to individual acts and attributes"—(U.S. QUARTERLY BOOK LIST, June, 1947).

"It is obviously the result of vast and prolonged labor and it is a vast and imposing piece of work"—(NEW YORK TIMES, March 1, 1942).

EVANS, BERGEN AND CORNELIA EVANS.
A Dictionary of Contemporary American Usage. New York: Random House, 1957. 567 p.

An alphabetically arranged list of grammatical and rhetorical terms, word usages, literary concepts, clichés, phrases, idioms, figures of speech, etc. "Informative and provocative."

FUNK, CHARLES E.
A Hog on Ice and Other Curious Expressions. New York: Harper & Brothers, 1955. 214 p.

Readable and amusing explanations of the origin of, for the most part, well known expressions, old and new.

The pleasing thing about Mr. Funk "is his willingness to turn his selections around slowly and have a look at them from all sides. . . . The reader will be amused almost always, surprised a good part of the time, and informed throughout"—(SAN FRANCISCO CHRONICLE, March 5, 1948).

Future lexicographers will acknowledge their indebtedness to the author for "the research he has done on old phrases and because he has set down in good time the origin of such modern phrases as "Behind the Eight Ball" and "Bronx Cheer"—(SATURDAY REVIEW OF LITERATURE, May 22, 1948).

GOLDIN, HYMAN E., FRANK O'LEARY, M. LIPSIUS.
Dictionary of American Underworld Lingo. New York: Twayne Publishers, Inc., 1950. 327 p.

Perhaps the most authentic work on the language of the underworld, written as it is, from the point of view of those who have had personal contact with the criminal.

Deliberately avoids any attempt to define linguistic origin. Its aim is rather "to provide a source book for students, writers, and law-enforcement agencies. It may even help the general reader to understand modern fiction"—(NEW YORK TIMES, Nov. 26, 1950).

JOHNSON, BURGES.
New Rhyming Dictionary and Poets' Handbook. Rev. ed. New York: Harper & Brothers, 1957. 464 p.

Part I of the first edition, published in 1931, constitutes a discussion of the basic forms of English and French verse. Part II of the first edition constitutes a rhyming dictionary, in three parts: (1) one-syllable rhymes; (2) two-syllable rhymes; (3) three-syllable rhymes. The 1957 edition contains some revision in the introductory sections, "Forms of English versification," and slight alterations and additions in the rhyming sections. There is a brief appendix.

KENYON, JOHN S. AND THOMAS ALBERT.
A Pronouncing Dictionary of American English. Springfield, Massachusetts: Merriam, 1949.

Aims to record the phonetic pronunciation of words in common use by the people who set the standards in each community. In addition to ordinary words, it also lists proper names, and also names in literature and history that are likely to be encountered by college students. If the word has only one pronunciation throughout America, only one phonetic spelling is given; if the word has more than one pronunciation, the regional differences are indicated.

"It will probably long hold its place as an indispensable handbook on American-English pronunciation, both for natives and foreigners"—(MODERN LANGUAGE NOTES, Dec. 1944).

"This book is of great interest and value. It allows for broad regional differences . . . lets you say a lot of things that the purist considers incorrect but that everybody has been saying for decades"—(NEW YORKER, 1944).

"A definite addition to the field"—(SUBSCRIPTION BOOKS BULLETIN, October, 1944).

MARCH, FRANCIS ANDREW AND FRANCIS A. MARCH, JR.
March's Thesaurus Dictionary. Issued under the editorial supervision of Norman Cousins. New Supplement by R. A. Goodwin. Garden City: Hanover House, 1958. 1240 p.

The 1925 edition defines over 200,000 words and phrases in the English language; differentiates between those which have found a place in language and those which have not. The New Supplement lists and defines "some 1,800 words and phrases which have come into general use since the turn of the century." The treatment and general format are the same as those employed in the basic volume, and the supplementary material, through the use of symbols and cross references, is integrated with the original.

NICHOLSON, MARGARET.
A Dictionary of American-English Usage, Based on Fowler's Modern English Usage. New York: Oxford University Press, 1957. 671 p.

A simplified version of Fowler's DICTIONARY OF MODERN USAGE, published in 1926. Some of the articles in Fowler's work are omitted, some are shortened, and new entries and illustrations are added. Hence Nicholson's work does not entirely replace the earlier one.

PARTRIDGE, ERIC.
Name Into Word: Proper Names that Have Become Common Property. New York: Macmillan, 1950.

Aims to list the names of persons, places, or things which have become so familiar that they are now accepted as having a symbolic meaning rather than a literal one; and are most likely to be met by the intelligent reader.

A "learned and enchanting work"—(NEW STATESMAN AND NATION, January, 1950).

A "delightful book," with virtually no important omissions—(SATURDAY REVIEW OF LITERATURE, April 15, 1950).

Provides "food for the philosopher and fun for the rest of us. It takes us behind the scenes"—(NEW YORK TIMES, Jan. 15, 1950).

A Dictionary of Clichés. New York: Macmillan Company, 1950.

An alphabetical arrangement of the ordinary cliches arranged into four groups: (1) "idioms that have become cliches"; (2) "Other hackneyed phrases"; (3) "Stock phrases and familiar quotations"; (4) "Quotations from English Literature."

Will "prove a delight to the scholarly reader and a terror to the writer of conscientious English"—(NATION, Nov. 23, 1940).

An "amusing, instructive, and valuable" work"—(NEW STATESMAN AND NATION, September 14, 1940).

"Mr. Partridge's . . . dictionary is informative, instructive, and great fun"—(NEW YORK TIMES, October 6, 1940).

A Dictionary of Forces' Slang, 1939–1945. London: Secker and Warburg, 1948. 212 p.

A single alphabet arrangement of navy, army, and air force slang.

A Dictionary of Slang and Unconventional English. New York: Macmillan, 1938. 1051 p.

An immense work which deals not only with slang, but with foul language as well, such as is found in many modern authors and in very few dictionaries. Many of the terms, in fact, are not even included in many of the slang dictionaries.

PEI, MARIO, FRANK GAYNOR.
A Dictionary of Linguistics. New York: Philosophical Library, 1954. 238 p.

Crisp and authoritative definitions of terms in virtually all fields of language study.

"Medium-sized and large libraries will want to add this useful work to their reference collection of special-purpose dictionaries"—(LIBRARY JOURNAL, September 15, 1954).

RADFORD, EDWIN.
Unusual Words and How They Came About. New York: Philosophical Library, 1946. 318 p.

An alphabetical arrangement of the meanings and origins of about 2,500 words and sayings which shed special light on customs and conventions of the age. Words and phrases which have entered the language as slang are excluded. Much of the matter is based, as the author acknowledges, on Brewer's DICTIONARY OF PHRASE AND FABLE.

ROGET, PETER MARK.
Roget's International Thesaurus: A Complete Book of Synonyms and Antonyms in American and British Usage. New York: Crowell, 1946. 1194 p.

A new edition of a standard work, first published in 1852; enlarged in 1879 by his son, John L. Roget; and again enlarged in 1911 by his grandson, Samuel Romilly Roget. The unique feature of the work is, as Roget himself noted, the arrangement of words, "not in alphabetical order as they are in a dictionary, but according to the ideas which they express."

Roget's Thesaurus of the English Language in Dictionary Form. Rev. and enl. by C. O. S. Mawson. New York: Garden City Books, 1936. 660 p.

A straight dictionary arrangement, in lieu of Roget's "idea" plan, with synonyms for all entries, but with more extensive lists of synonyms for the principal entries. Also contains a comprehensive group of foreign words and phrases frequently found in English, with their definitions.

Thesaurus of English Words and Phrases. Rev. by D. C. Browning. New York: E. P. Dutton & Company, 1953. 600 p.

Follows the original "idea" plan, but has a new numbering system which facilitates the location of every word. A complete revision which deletes obsolete words and adds many new words, including slang, Americanisms, and technical terms.

SCHWARTZ, ROBERT J.
The Complete Dictionary of Abbreviations. New York: Thomas Y. Crowell Company, 1955. 211 p.

About 25,000 abbreviations employed in virtually every field—business, law, science, music, government; as well as abbreviations of the names of colleges and universities and of the companies used in stock-market quotations. The appendix contains a list of signs and symbols.

SHANKLE, George Earlie.
Current Abbreviations. New York: The H. W. Wilson Company, 1944. 207 p.

A fairly comprehensive alphabetical list of abbreviations—music, science, technology, government, and others. The Greek letter fraternities are alphabetized at the end of the appropriate English letter in accordance with the English spelling of the Greek initial.

STEVENSON, Herbert J.
Abbreviations: A Dictionary of Abbreviations. New York: Macmillan, 1943. 126 p.

Attempts to include the most common abbreviations used. The main division lists alphabetically some 7,500 general abbreviations. A second division lists the abbreviations under special fields,—Books of the Bible; Shakespeare's works; Legal Literature; Christian Names; Geography, etc.

"Without laughing off the obvious value of Abbreviations to chaps who are thrown for a loss by the other man's shop talk and verbal short cuts, any reviewer should certainly recommend it also for rainy-day reading"—(SPRINGFIELD REPUBLICAN, September 9, 1943).

"Within the limits set the book has been well done, but it is not exhaustive"—(NEW YORK TIMES, November 7, 1943).

WALKER, John.
Rhyming Dictionary of the English Language, rev. and enl. by L. H. Dawson. New York: E. P. Dutton & Company, 1924. 549 p.

First compiled in 1775, revised and enlarged by J. Longmuir in 1865, and reprinted many times, the RHYMING DICTIONARY includes over 54,000 entries, arranged according to final vowel sounds. The index lists "allowable rhymes" according to combinations of vowels and consonants.

"Here is a new edition of a standard work as indispensable to poets as Roget's THESAURUS. Here is the whole English language arranged according to its terminations. . . . We welcome this valuable old book in its new spruce dress. It is one of the volumes that are necessary to every complete reference shelf"—(SATURDAY REVIEW OF LITURATURE, January 3, 1929).

WEINGARTEN, JOSEPH ABRAHAM.
An American Dictionary of Slang and Colloquial Speech. New York: Privately printed, 1954. 390 p.

Attempts to give and to authenticate the earliest date for each word and phrase.

WENTWORTH, HAROLD.
American Dialect Dictionary. New York: Crowell, 1944. 747 p.

A comprehensive list of well over 10,000 terms, dealing mainly, as is noted in the "Preface," with "dialect in the sense of localisms, regionalisms, and provincialisms; folk speech, urban as well as rustic New England and Southern United States dialects viewed in their deviations from General Northern or Western. . . ."

"The author is a well known lexicographer and philologist and has lived and studied the subject in all of the regions from which the three main dialect classifications stem. This should prove a valuable reference item"—(KIRKUS, July 1, 1944).

"An excellent dictionary of homely folk speech of America. Mr. Wentworth's editing shows that he is a competent lexicographer. He has brought a mass of loose material into an easily managed order. . . . It will be very useful to students of dialect and to writers of tales and will provide a fine stimulus to further studies"—(NEW YORK TIMES, July 23, 1944).

WHITFIELD, JANE SHAW.
The Improved Rhyming Dictionary. New York: Crowell, 1951. 283 p.

A list of about 115,000 words, arranged under main headings according to general meanings. Particularly useful for the inclusion of recent words, slang, and foreign words.

WOOD, CLEMENT.
Wood's Unabridged Rhyming Dictionary. Cleveland: The World Publishing Company, 1943. 1049 p.

An arrangement of single, double, and triple rhymes according to sound, rather than spelling. The introduction discusses the mechanics and forms of poetry.

ENCYCLOPEDIAS

Encyclopedia Americana. New York: Encyclopedia Americana Corporation, 1949. 30 vols.

Aims to present "Knowledge with faithfulness and with scholarly impartiality, avoiding the promotion of theories and such discussions and defenses as are entirely foreign to the character and nature of an encyclopedia . . . to present in an intelligent and informing way, the history and nature of the civilization, institutions, systems, activities, and achievements of mankind with sufficient usefulness to furnish the general reader a fair and adequate understanding of the development of man and his social life" – (Pref.).

Although it has a large number of relatively short entries, with special emphasis upon personal and place names, it is notable for the long essay-type treatment of major topics, most of which are followed by comparatively extensive bibliographies; and also for its exceptionally thorough biographical coverage of eminent Americans and Canadians, especially of the nineteenth century and earlier.

Keeping the AMERICANA up-to-date is the AMERICANA ANNUAL: AN ENCYCLOPEDIA OF CURRENT EVENTS, which summarizes the events of the preceding year and, in format, resembles the volumes of the encyclopedia.

Encyclopedia Britannica. Chicago: Encyclopedia Britannica, 1949. 24 vols.

The oldest, largest, and most famous of the English-language encyclopedias, aiming, as is noted in the fourteenth edition, "to provide the fullest, most various digest of universal information.

The first eight editions are now of virtually no use; but the ninth, eleventh, and fourteenth editions and their supplements must still be used: the ninth, "the high-water mark of the Britannica, for subjects where recent information is not of primary importance; the eleventh, because, though more popular than earlier editions, it is nonetheless a scholarly and carefully edited work, and retains a preference for greater length and comprehensiveness; and the fourteenth because of its up-to-dateness and its greater number of more popular entries.

The main text is comprised by the first 23 volumes; the detailed index, always to be used if one wishes to find all the pertinent material, is embraced by volume 24.

Since 1938, the BRITANNICA has issued a BRITANNICA BOOK OF THE YEAR to cover the events and developments of the preceding year and to keep the work as up-to-date as it can. Each volume contains a cumulative index to that volume and the four preceding ones, as well as a subject index to illustrations.

Speaking of the ninth edition, the reviewer notes that the work, from being a mere compilation, has "become a work of national importance, containing original treatises on science, art, and literature by famous literary and scientific men"—(NATURE, 1875).

The eleventh edition is referred to as a "work of transcendent merit, one unapproached by any similar publication"—(NATION, May 25, 1911).

"The most famous and best reference work in the English language. Complete in every sense"—(SATURDAY REVIEW OF LITERATURE).

Encyclopedia of Social Sciences. New York: The Macmillan Company, 1930–1935. 15 vols.

Designed to appeal to three groups, scholars, "intelligentia," and the general public by: (1) providing a synopsis of the progress which has been made in the general areas of the social sciences; (2) assembling those salient facts which will assist those who wish to keep abreast of the most recent investigation and accomplishment; (3) constituting a center of authoritative knowledge for the creation of a sounder and more informed public opinion on problems central to the foundation of social progress and world development.

The first attempt to embrace the entire field of the social sciences. All articles are by specialists, are fully signed, and are followed by bibliographies which are generally adequate.

". . . is another milestone marking the progress of the sciences that seek an understanding of man, and another achievement of American scholarship"—(NATION, Feb. 5, 1930).

". . . a compendium of completed discovery which will for years remain a standard of information . . ."—(THE NEW REPUBLIC, Aug. 30, 1930).

"Taken as a whole the encyclopedia may be said to represent the highest standards of scholarship. . . . Viewed in its entirety, the encyclopedia is the best possible refutation of those who say that the study of man cannot be scientific"—(THE NATION, Sept. 25, 1935).

"Save for minor gaps . . . there seems to be no doubt that these 15 imposing volumes will hold their place for a long time as a definitive exhibit of the content and scope of American and international cooperation in a large intellectual field"—(NEW YORK TIMES, August 11, 1935).

Catholic Encyclopedia: An International Work of Reference on the Constitution, Doctrine, Discipline and History of the Catholic Church. New York: Catholic Encyclopedia, 1907–1914. 16 vols. Supplement I, 1922; Supplement II, 1950–1954.

"It differs from the general encyclopedia in omitting facts and information which have no relation to the Church. On the other hand it is not exclusively a church encyclopedia, nor is it limited to the ecclesiastical sciences and the doings of churchmen. It records all that Catholics have done, not only in behalf of charity and morals, but also for the intellectual and artistic development of mankind"—(Preface).

A work of solid scholarship with signed articles which, in the main, are by the most eminent authorities, with adequate bibliographies and illustrations. Especially useful for questions dealing with medieval history, literature, philosophy, art, and early Church history.

Although the supplements have brought some of the material in the basic work up to date, the main volumes are generally in need of revision.

"The work for reference to Catholic institution, doctrine, discipline, and history of the Catholic Church . . . a most excellent work"—(EXTENSION MAGAZINE).

"In the matter of form" the articles are "models of what encyclopedic articles should be . . . it contains a great deal of interest to every intelligent man, and, so far as it is used by non-Catholics, must contribute to the correcting of erroneous opinions and the breaking down of prejudices"—(THE NATION, June 20, 1907).

Collier's Encyclopedia. New York: P. F. Collier & Son Corporation, 1950 —. 20 vols.

More advanced than the juvenile encyclopedias, but neither so broad in scope nor so scholarly in treatment as the BRITANNICA and AMERICANA; principally aimed at the junior college level. Articles are contributed by specialists and are initialed, with the full names and positions of the authors given at the beginning of volume 1. A special feature of the encyclopedia is the 140 page briefly annotated bibliography section in the final volume.

THE COLLIER'S YEARBOOK, originally prepared as a supplement to the NATIONAL ENCYCLOPEDIA and called the NATIONAL YEARBOOK, is designed to serve both as a supplement to COLLIER'S ENCLCLOPEDIA, and as an annual survey. Since becoming a supplement to COLLIER'S ENCYCLOPEDIA, it has become increasingly more like it in scope and format.

Chamber's Encyclopedia. New ed. London: Oxford University Press, 1950. 15 vols.

A new edition of a famous old encyclopedia, probably the most respected general reference work published in England. Its format is different from the old edition; its articles and length of treatment are different. It is meant for the "educated layman who has some general grounding in a variety of subjects from which he can proceed to more exact and detailed information in a special field.

The articles are generally, as in the previous editions, brief and devoted to specific topics, but a number are on broader topics and more extensive in form. Most of the articles are initialed and have adequate bibliographies. Since the emphasis is on matters of special interest to Britons, in which area the treatment is generally fuller than that in other encyclopedias, CHAMBER'S ENCYCLOPEDIA constitutes an important supplement.

Jewish Enclyclopedia: A Descriptive Record of the History, Religion, Literature, and Customs of the Jewish people from the earliest times to the present day. New York: Funk and Wagnalls Company, 1901–1906. 12 vols.

A scholarly work which, though somewhat dated, is still valuable for its biographies, its descriptions of the present state of Jews throughout the world, and for its elucidations of Talmudic law.

On the one hand it is a true encyclopedia, viewing always from the Jewish viewpoint; on the other hand, "it is a cyclopaedia as the record of a single branch of knowledge—the civilization of a single race . . .—(NATION).

"The articles on folk-lore, manners, and customs, superstitions—Jewish life and thought on its ordinary levels—are eminently to the point and . . . form a mass of information nowhere else so accessible"—(NATION, October 2, 1902).

Universal Jewish Encyclopedia: An Authoritative and Popular Presentation of Jews and Judaism since the earliest times. New York: Universal Jewish Encyclopedia, Inc., 1939–1944. 10 vols.

A more popular treatment than the JEWISH ENCYCLOPEDIA covering virtually every phase of Judaism and Jewish life, history, religion, and culture, especially impressive in its treatment of American Subjects. Most of the entries are signed by specialists and many of the articles are followed by bibliographies. Admirably supplements, not supersedes the more scholarly work.

New International Encyclopedia. New York: Dodd, Mead & Company, 1902–1930. 23 vols.

Once the first choice of many librarians and bibliographers, it is now, because unfortunately out of date, useful only for articles on subjects which do not require revision. Important articles are by specialists; minor articles, by staff members. Articles are unsigned, but a list of the authors of the main articles appears at the beginning of each volume. A special feature is the inclusion of many biographical articles, some 20,000 in all, principally of Americans of both continents, and its excellent bibliographies.

THE NEW INTERNATIONAL YEARBOOK originally published as INTERNATIONAL YEARBOOK is published as a compendium of the world's progress for the preceding year and also serves as a supplement for the encyclopedia.

Written "throughout by competent persons acting under the direction of a very able editorial staff; it is the result of a critical study of all the famous works of reference which have at any time appeared in Europe or the United States; and it combines the four qualities which are necessary to make up the ideal encyclopedia"—(THE AMERICAN CATHOLIC QUARTERLY REVIEW, July, 1904).

LITERARY HANDBOOKS

In addition to the general literary handbooks, the English major should seek familiarity with the many author handbooks, four of the more representative of which are included in this section.

ALDEN, RAYMOND M.
A Shakespeare Handbook. New York: Crofts, 1925. 240 p.

A very useful collection of Shakespeare source material, obviating the need of going to the volumes of Holinshed, Plutarch, Bandillo and the others. Contains the known facts of Shakespeare's life, the chronology of his plays, source material (the main portion of the work), and notes on grammar and versification.

"Shakespeare's lovers and a large number of intelligent readers who wish to join the ranks will find this little volume greatly to their taste"—(EDUCATION REVIEW, October, 1925).

"The book makes available for the student material which will aid him alike in analyzing the structures of the plays and in appreciating the genius with which the dramatist transformed his borrowed plots and characters"—(SPRINGFIELD REPUBLICAN, 1925).

"This useful little book will be helpful to teachers and for self-education. It aims to give students of collegiate grade and other mature, but not learned, readers the materials needed for the study of Shakespeare's principal works"—(WISCONSIN LIBRARY BULLETIN, October, 1925).

BARNHART, CLARENCE L. AND WILLIAM HALSEY.
The New Century Handbook of English Literature. New York: Appleton-Century-Crofts, Inc., 1956. 1157 p.

More than 14,000 entries, arranged alphabetically, with pronunciation, and covering Anglo-American, Canadian, Australian, Irish, and South African works of literature. Essentially based upon THE NEW CENTURY CYCLOPEDIA OF NAMES, differ-

ing most importantly from it in possessing a greater number of entries dealing with literary forms and other matters not properly falling under the category of "name." A comprehensive collection of data on major literary works, characters, movements, etc., seeking to answer questions most likely to be asked by modern American readers of English literature.

"The publication of a major new reference work is an uncommon event, and especially welcome when that work is of high quality. Clarence Barnhart is an experienced editor of books of reference, and the latest work to bear his name comes well up to expectations"—(BOOKLIST, April 15, 1956).

"Here 'English' means 'not American,' rather than 'English only'. . . . Even American scholars of English literature appear (M. M. Manly of Chicago). But Emerson, Poe, Lowell, and other American men of letters, however influential or active they were in Britain, are out. . . . There is no other reference work which has the same timeliness, scale, and scope as this"—(CHICAGO SUNDAY TRIBUNE, March 18, 1956).

"Throughout the book there is evidence of careful editing and scholarly selection of terms"—(BOOKLIST, October 1, 1956).

BARON, JOSEPH L.
A Treasury of Jewish Citations. New York: Crown Publishers, Inc., 1956. 700 p.

Some 18,000 quotations by or about Jews, in some 1,000 categories, ranging from "Ability" to "Zionism." Many of the quotations are familiar ones, but literally thousands of the striking quotations are from relatively little known persons. Each quotation is identified by author, title of the work, and date. Has an author and subject index.

"Many of the proverbs, maxims, and comments—which cover the secular and religious world of ancient and contemporary Judaism—have never before been translated into English. . . . Of particular value to speakers and students"—(BOOKLIST, September 8, 1956).

". . . it will be a useful reference work as well as a fascinating introduction to Jewish thought. 'Of the making of books there is no end,' but this one is recommended for any public or college library"—(LIBRARY JOURNAL, June 1, 1956).

BARTLETT, JOHN.
Familiar Quotations. A Collection of Passages, Phrases and Proverbs Traced to Their Sources in Ancient and Modern Literature. 13th ed. Boston: Little, Brown & Company, 1955. 1068 p.

A standard guide to quotations, containing some 113,500 entries, arranged by authors according to the order of their birth dates. The index is so thorough that often even a vague recollection of the passages is sufficient to reveal the quotation sought after.

The publishers of the eleventh edition noted that for every two quotations added at least one was eliminated. Hence there are times when the tenth edition will still be useful.

"What Bartlett needs now is to have its splendid grab-bag of riches winnowed and put in order by a touch of scholarship"—(TIME, December 13, 1948).

Of the twelfth edition it was noted: The "first half, through Kipling, is unchanged; the remainder is re-edited and enlarged, with quotations of the war years added, as well as more translations from other languages"—(BOOKLIST, December 15, 1948).

"This famous collection of passages, phrases, and proverbs . . . has long been a standby of the library. . . . Bartlett has always been noted for readability; the new edition keeps up to this standard"—(NEW YORK HERALD TRIBUNE, December 19, 1948).

BREWER, EBENEZER COBHAM.
Reader's Handbook of Famous Names in Fiction, Allusions, References, Proverbs, Plots, Stories, and Poems. Philadelphia: Lippincott, 1898. 1501 p.

Aims to furnish the reader with a brief and lucid account of the words used in references and allusions by poets and prose writers, as well as to furnish information about plots of dramas, tales, and narrative poems. The appendixes contain: (1) List of English authors and their works; (2) Title list of dramas and operas, giving authors and dates. Later issues of the work lack the appendixes.

"Those readers who remember with affection Brewer's little red READER'S HANDBOOK will relish Mr. Benet's new reference book for readers"—(NEW YORK TIMES, November 7, 1948).

BREWER, Ebenezer Cobham.
Brewer's Dictionary of Phrase and Fable. Rev. and enl. ed. New York: Harper & Brothers, 1952. 977 p.
The most recent edition of a work which in England and America has become one of the classic reference works, expanded and brought fully up-to-date by the addition of newer material, those that were fostered by World War II.

The scope of the work is amply indicated by the lengthy subtitle: "giving illustrative quotations from the works of the most famous authors from the earliest time to the present day; a history of the chief figures mentioned in the mythologies of the world; a record of superstitions and customs, ancient and modern; an explanation of phrases commonly in use in the English language, of native origin or borrowed from other tongues; ancient cant and contemporary slang, with their equivalents in others languages of Europe; the stories of well-known characters from novels and romances; local and national legends; a glossary of scientific, historical, political, and archaeological terms and events; references bearing on every description of economic and scientific data; etymological and much other information."

BURACH, A. E.
The Writer's Handbook: A Complete Reference Library for Free-Lance Writers. Boston: The Writer, Inc., 1957. 650 p.
Contains 79 chapters of instruction by leading authors and editors on every field of writing, craft and commercial phases; 1,000 markets for stories, plays, articles, and other literary productions.

". . . contains a wealth of information of great value to the aspiring writers regardless of what branch of literature he is interested in" – (Boston Transcript, Jan. 1937).

"Textbook for the literary novice containing articles on various types of professional writing. . . . Most of the articles have appeared in the magazine The Writer during the last two years" – (Book Review Digest, 1937).

CLARK, Barrett Harper.
Study of the Modern Drama: A Handbook for the Study and Appreciation of the Best Plays, European, English and Ameri-

can, of the Last Century. New ed. New York: Appleton, 1928. 535 p.

Separate chapters on Norwegian, German, French, Italian, English, Irish, and American drama, giving salient facts about the major plays.

"In spite of easily remediable limitations, this book takes its place at once as the best existing survey of modern European and American dramatic movements"—(SPECTATOR, April 18, 1925).

"A student of modern drama would go far to find a more careful and detailed guide book"—(THEATRE ARTS, July, 1925).

"The author's selections are judicious and representative; his treatment impartial"—(CATHOLIC WORLD, June, 1925).

BURKE, W. J. AND W. D. HOWE.
American Authors and Books, 1640–1940. New York: Gramercy Publishing Co., 1943. 858 p.

The aim is to present "the most useful facts about the writing, illustrating, editing, publishing, reviewing, collecting, selling and preservation of American books from 1640 to 1940"—(Preface).

A quick reference tool, somewhat similar to the OXFORD COMPANION TO AMERICAN LITERATURE with larger coverage but briefer articles. Author, title, fictional characters, magazines, newspapers, places, names, and other entries are alphabetically arranged with cross references. Limited to continental United States.

"Contains much useful material not hereto readily available . . . . a veritable storehouse of information for journalists, writers, teachers and others actively interested in American literature. Comprehensive and accurate, and includes many hundreds of items which the author does not suggest"—(BOOK WEEK, July, 1949).

DEVANE, WILLIAM CLYDE.
Browning Handbook. New York: Appleton, Century-Crofts, Inc., 1955. 590 p.

The main divisions are: Life, Early Poems, Middle Years, and Last Decade. Biography, publication facts, and critical discussions.

"In addition to gathering up the results of Browning's scholarship to date, Mr. DeVane has made contributions of his own, notably in regard to the source of the descriptive passage in 'Childe Roland, in Lairesse's 'The Art of Painting in All Its Branches,' and in the connection between Browning's 'Fifine at the Fair' and Rossetti's 'Jenney' "—(NEW REPUBLIC, December, 935).

"A contribution of exceptional value to Browning study. . . . The new handbook impresses one as a work essential to the student or critical reader"—(SPRINGFIELD REPUBLICAN, July, 1935).

DIXON, RAYMOND J.

Granger's Index to Poetry. 4th ed.; rev. and enl. New York: Columbia University Press, 1953. 1869 p.

Essentially a key to the contents of those anthologies most commonly found in libraries. Indexes poems from 577 anthologies. The two principal innovations in this edition of a standard work are: (1) the combination into a single Title and First Line Index of The Title Index and First Line Index; and (2) the addition of a Subject Index.

A Supplement, 1951–1955, edited by Raymond J. Dixon, and published by Columbia University Press in 1957, indexes poems from 88 anthologies. Some 70,000 entries are arranged by title and first line, and contains an author and subject index.

Of the first edition, published by McClurg, it was noted: "The college girl [Edith Granger] has set a high example of originality, intelligence, laboriousness and accuracy . . . We are glad to observe that future editions are contemplated"—(THE NATION, September 22, 1904).

GHOSH, JYOTISH CHANDRA.

Annals of English Literature, 1475–1925. The Principal Publications of Each Year with an Alphabetical Index of Authors and Their Works. Oxford: Clarendon Press, 1935. 340 p.

A chronological list, providing year by year the authors and titles of publications, with general descriptions; marginal notes indicate contemporary foreign publications, or events of biographical importance. A detailed author index.

"The book is as practical a small work of reference as has

been issued in a long time"—(COMMONWEAL, March 20, 1936).

"Sound in scholarship and admirable in the organization of its vast contents"—(NEW YORK TIMES, March 15, 1936).

"It is not exaggeration to say that the compilers of this little reference book have put every student of English literature in their debt"—(SPECTATOR, February 21, 1936).

"The book can be used equally through the approach of the authors . . . and also through the approach of the years . . . . it can be read straightforward, with both profit and pleasure; and it can be worked backwards from the index in the process of checking dates of authors and of books"—(TIMES LITERARY SUPPLEMENT, February 1, 1936).

HALLIDAY, FRANK.

A Shakespeare Companion, 1550–1950. New York: Funk & Wagnalls Company, 1952. 742 p.

Interesting and very readable information about the playwright and his contemporaries. All entries are alphabetically arranged: life, critical studies of Shakespeare, biographical data on his friends, printers, publishers, players, etc.; critical notes on poems, productions. A useful bibliography. For the reader and general student, rather than for the scholar.

HANFORD, JAMES HOLLY.

A Milton Handbook. 4th ed. New York: Crofts, 1946. 465 p.

A companion to Milton studies for the advanced student. The new addition contains a new appendix on Milton in Italy and textual revisions and additions based upon recent research, as well as fuller footnotes and bibliographies.

HARSH, PHILIP WHALEY.

A Handbook of Classical Drama. Stanford, California: Stanford University Press, 1956. 526 p.

Discussions of the structure, purpose, and meaning of 45 Greek and 36 Latin plays, aiming to constitute "a modern appreciation of the plays as literature and a convenient brief guide to further critical material." In five parts: GREEK TRAGEDY: Aeschylus, Sophocles, Euripides; OLD COMEDY: Aristophanes; NEW COMEDY: Menander; ROMAN COMEDY: Plautus, Terence; ROMAN TRAGEDY: Seneca. An extensive bibliography and a very detailed index.

". . . deserves high praise . . . is a guide that gives relevant facts accurately and conveniently"—(BOOK WEEK, January 21, 1945).

". . . indispensable for any student of the theater. . . . Very highly recommended"—(CLASSICAL PHILOLOGY, July, 1945).

". . . is meant for reference and as such will be found useful to students and to the scholars in the field"—(LIBRARY JOURNAL, July, 1944).

HART, JAMES D.

The Oxford Companion to American Literature. 3d ed. New York: Oxford University Press, 1956. 890 p.

A chronological arrangement of "short biographies, and bibliographies of American authors, with information regarding their style and subject matter; nearly 900 summaries and descriptions of the important American novels, stories, essays, poems and plays; definitions and historical outlines of literary schools and movements; and information on literary societies, magazines, anthologies, co-operative publications, literary awards, book collectors, printers, etc."—(Preface).

A special feature is the chronological index, a year-by-year outline, giving in parallel columns the literary and social events from 1000 to 1947.

HARTNOLL, PHYLLIS.

The Oxford Companion to the Theatre. London: Oxford University Press, 1957. 887 p.

A reprint of the first edition, published in 1951, with the addition of a thirty-two page supplement and one hundred and fifty photographic illustrations. International in scope and comprehensively historical. Emphasizes the popular, rather than the literary theater, and the actor, rather than the playwright. Devotes one article to opera and one to ballet; does not cover the cinema.

HARVEY, SIR PAUL.
The Oxford Companion to English Literature. 3d ed. Oxford: Clarendon Press, 1946. 940 p.

An alphabetical arrangement of brief articles on authors' lives, pseudonyms, characters in fiction, plots of novels and plays, famous works, places in literature, allusions. Includes a small number of American authors; many bibliographies.

"For here is collected a vast amount of information which should, but all too rarely does, form the equipement of the cultured reader, conveniently arranged, and catholic enough in scope to meet a wide variety of needs"—(SATURDAY REVIEW, April 18, 1933).

"Published as a literary reference book, it will be of service to editors, teachers, and librarians"—(NEW REPUBLIC, March 8, 1933).

HARVEY, SIR PAUL.
The Oxford Companion to Classical Literature. Oxford: Clarendon Press, 1937. 468 p.

Basically the same in principle as the companion volume on English literature, with the same single alphabetical arrangement.

A useful handbook of concise information on the principal classical authors and their works, with as much background data as is necessary to render the works intelligible.

GRAHAM, BESSIE.
Bookman's Manual: A Guide to Literature. 8th ed. rev. and enl. by Hester R. Hoffman. New York: Bowker, 1958. 987 p.

Designed primarily for use by booksellers and librarians, but is of value to anyone as a general guide to basic works in a wide variety of fields, frequently with useful annotations.

"The new chapter on Greek and Roman Classics in Translation has replaced the old chapter on Classics in Translation. . . . The chapter on Bibles, perhaps the most widely used by booksellers, has a more thorough listing of the publications of the Bible Publishing Houses. . . . The last section on the

Sacred Books of Other Religions has been enlarged. . . . A new section on The Authorship Controversy appears in the chapter on William Shakespeare because of the number of recent books of interest to the general reader on this perennial question long debated. . . . The two formerly separate chapters on Biography, and Autobiography and Journals have now been combined into one chapter on Biography and Autobiography. . . . The chapter on Travel has become a chapter on Travel and Adventure . . ."—(Preface).

Upon the appearance of the sixth edition, the reviewer noted: "There can be no doubt of the fact that this monumental work is of inestimable value to both booksellers and librarians, and that the new edition will be welcomed by members of both professions"—(LIBRARY JOURNAL, August 1, 1948).

MOSSE, FERNAND.
Handbook of Middle English. Baltimore: The Johns Hopkins Press, 1952.

"This admirable work (long introductions, texts, notes, glossary and reproductions of manuscripts) should . . . greatly benefit medieval English studies in French universities. The author insists on 'phonetic reality,' cites originals where and when they are known, assumes a knowledge of Old English, verifies all the texts, and omits diacritics save in the earliest. . . . There are however serious blemishes. Many misprints, wrongly numbered references, and wavering punctuation must be added to the already lengthy errata though some mis-spellings will not deceive the student . . ."—(REVIEW OF ENGLISH STUDIES, January, 1951).

SMITH, WILLIAM GEORGE.
Oxford Dictionary of English Proverbs. 2d. ed. rev. by Sir Paul Harvey. Oxford: Clarendon Press, 1948. 740 p.

Planned on the lines of the O.E.D., with each proverb illustrated by dated quotations. The first edition (1935) contained approximately 10,000 proverbs, arranged alphabetically by first word, including the article. The second edition contains about

11,000 proverbs, arranged alphabetically according to the first significant word, with preceding words, if any, generally transferred to the end.

PATRICK, DAVID.
Chamber's Cyclopedia of English Literature. rev. by J. L. Geddie. Philadelphia: Lippincott, 1922–38. 3 vols.

A chronological arrangement, containing many articles on individual writers, some on literary forms, periods, and subjects. For each author treated, gives brief biography, comment on, and specimens of, his writings, a bibliography, and, in some instances, a portrait. Volume 3 consists of an author-title index.

"The revision of the material covering the late 19th and 20th centuries seems, in proportion to the broad scope of the work, sufficient to bring the set up to date, although more comprehensive discussion of the contemporary literature of the British overseas dominions and of the United States would have been desirable . . . . is recommended"—(SUBSCRIPTION BOOKS BULLETIN, April, 1939).

"The new edition . . . is the result of a conservative revision which has left unchanged the size, proportion, and special characteristics of the work while changing articles for essential accuracy and up-to-dateness. . . . The large library should find it useful"—(LIBRARY JOURNAL, 49:17).

ROSE, HERBERT JENNINGS.
Handbook of Greek Literature: From Homer to the Age of Lucian. 2d. ed. New York: E. P. Dutton, Inc., 1942. 454 p.

Aims to survey the entire field of Greek literature and to embrace the findings of the latest investigations on the subject. Social backgrounds and influences, as well as writers and their works are analyzed. In chapter form, with a very detailed index.

Professor Rose has covered Greek literature "not only comprehensively but with a wealth of criticism that will prove richly rewarding to the reader. . . . Because it is not a mere summary of literary trends and attainments, but embodies a penetrating commentary, Professor Rose's new volume is certain to recommend itself highly to students"—(NEW YORK TIMES, December 15, 1935).

". . . a brief but inclusive survey of developments from Homer to Lucian"—(BOOK REVIEW DIGEST, 1935).

SOBEL, BERNARD.
The Theater Handbook and Digest of Plays. New York: Crown Publishers, 1948. 897 p.

A single alphabet arrangement of theatrical terms, biographical notices, synopsis of almost 1,000 plays, playwrights, producers, and brief essays, many of them signed, by specialists on specific phases of drama or theater. The addenda includes a bibliography and a subject index of plays.

"Should prove extremely useful despite the fact that it is not clear just what principles of inclusion and exclusion were adopted in compiling a 900-page encyclopedia of the theater of all time"—(NATION, Jan. 13, 1940).

"Mistakes are inevitable in an undertaking of this kind, and omissions as well . . . but the book has a breezy, theatrical quality of its own, combining the casual and the eternal, . . . and it serves well its double purpose of providing information and entertainment"—(THEATER ART, Feb., 1940).

"At last a revised edition in compact and handy form of one of the most useful theatre handbooks available. The biographies have been rewritten and brought up to date and are of considerable value. . . ."—(LIBRARY JOURNAL, December, 1948).

"An excellent reference compiled by a distinguished laborer in the Broadway vineyard"—(SATURDAY REVIEW OF LITERATURE, October 30, 1948).

"The style is lively, the facts are accurate and well-indexed as anybody could hope for"—(THEATRE ARTS, October, 1948).

TAVENNER, BLAIR.
Brief Facts: A Concise Handbook of Useful Information for the Student, Traveler, Writer, Teacher, Librarian, Speaker, Business Man and General Reader. New York: Putnam's Sons, 1936. 941 p.

Partial contents: Battles; Bible Characters; Colleges and Universities; First Aid Rules; Geologic History of the Earth; Inventions and Discoveries; Mathematical Tables; Mountain Ranges; Mythological Characters; Natural Wonders; Operas;

Rulers of England; Sport Records; Stars and Constellations; State Flowers and Birds; Weights and Measures and World War Outlines.

"The facts filling this book are indeed briefly stated, but there is such an outstanding number and variety of them that as the reader looks through the pages he feels more and more overwhelmed, almost awed. By the herculean labor of collecting, sorting, and arranging them, Mr. Tavenner has done a big job very efficiently, and has provided a book that ought to prove extremely useful to anybody"—(BOOK REVIEW DIGEST, 1936).

THRALL, WILLIAM F. AND A. HIBBARD.
A Handbook to Literature. New York: Doubleday Doran & Company, Inc., 1936.

Aims to provide for students of English and American literature the most important items in the framework of their interests. Grouping: alphabetical listing of terms, giving brief explanations; brief discussions of historical periods. The Appendix contains in chronological order an outline of English and American literature.

". . . an excellent handbook. The authors have surely succeeded in the one major object they had in mind, 'to make readily clear to those engaged in the study of English and American literature the most important items in the framework of their studies' "—(NEW YORK TIMES, June 14, 1936).

"A book which should prove a very ready help in trouble"—(SATURDAY REVIEW OF LITERATURE, June 13, 1936).

WALSH, WILLIAM S.
Handy Book of Literary Curiosities. Philadelphia: J. B. Lippincott Company, 1893, 1925. 1104 p.

A useful and entertaining collection of items generally not found in the usual reference work,—plagiarisms, literary forgeries, puns, riddles, and others.

"The tracing of analogies or finding of parallelisms for familiar quotations has especially engaged the author's zeal, and proverbs and slang have next received his attention, while under a large number of general titles he has stored away a mass of anecdote, fact and fancy beyond the reach of his index of cross references." Some of the material we "could easily have dispensed with, but we preferred to have it rather than to part with it for occasional reference"—(THE NATION, January 5, 1893).

WESSEN, MAURICE H.

Crowell's Dictionary of English Grammar: A Handbook of American Usage. New York: Thomas Y. Crowell Company, 1928. 703 p.

Essentially a guide to variations between English and American idiom. All entries are alphabetically arranged and treated briefly—parts of speech and their uses, syntax, synonyms, idioms, homonyms, slang, colloquialisms, errors of speech and of grammatical constructions.

"The principal virtues of the volume are simplicity and completeness." The book is "simultaneously a guide to grammatical correctness, a dictionary of grammatical terms, a list of words and constructions to avoid, a compendium of current slang, and a stylebook of contemporary usage. His work should prove of great service to students, editors, proofreaders and young writers"—(BOOKLIST, July, 1928).

ANTHOLOGIES AND HISTORIES

Anthologies

ALDERMAN, E. A. AND J. C. HARRIS.
Library of Southern Literature. New Orleans: Martin and Hoyt, 1908–1923. 17 vols.

The first thirteen volumes contain the biographical and critical sketches, and selected extracts arranged alphabetically according to the authors covered. The fourteenth volume comprises miscellanea,—poems, anecdotes, letters, epitaphs, and inscriptions, quotations, bibliography. Volume fifteen is a biographical dictionary, containing 3800 sketches. Volume sixteen constitutes a handbook of supplementary historical reading, as well as references to the bibliographies in the first thirteen volumes, and the supplementary lists; index of authors, titles, and subjects. Volume seventeen is a Supplement.

BENET, W. R. AND H. N. PEARSON.
Oxford Anthology of American Literature: An Historical Selection of Verse and Prose Arranged Chronologically. New York: Oxford University Press, 1938. 2 vols.

Volume One, John Smith to Abraham Lincoln; Volume Two, Walt Whitman to the Present.

Contains an alphabetical index of authors, first lines, and titles, as well as biographical and bibliographical data. The separate bibliography following the Commentary is divided into two parts: Historical, Social and Intellectual Background; and Literary History and Criticism.

"The worth of such a volume is entirely dependent upon the conscience and literary taste of its editors"; whence the work "is most fortunate, for William Rose Benet and Norman Holmes Pearson planned and executed it with great care and intelligence. . . . Their judgment was admirable, and the most essential examples of creative writing have been fitted into the general pattern of our intellectual development"—(NEW YORK TIMES, December 25, 1938).

"Arguing with a pair of anthologists who admit everything beforehand makes little sense. Fortunately, their volume represents so Catholic a taste that probably a few specialists will find much to carp at and most readers will find much to delight them"—(YALE REVIEW, Spring, 1939).

"This book provides ample evidence of the usefulness of intelligence and sound scholarship in making an anthology. Principles guided the construction of this book, though the statement of these principles in the preface is much fuzzier than that made by the selections themselves and in the commentaries"—(YALE REVIEW, Spring, 1939).

BRYANT, WILLIAM CULLEN.
New Library of Poetry and Song; rev. and enl. with recent authors and containing a dictionary of poetical quotations. New York: Baker, 1903. 1100 p.

"The marked success of A LIBRARY OF POETRY AND SONG, as issued in the year 1870, showed that the work supplied a real popular need. Since the date of its publication, between seventy and eighty thousand copies of the book have been taken by the public whose confidence in the name of Mr. Bryant, as its editor, has been borne out by the work itself. . . . Great pains have been taken to insure the correctness of the text with a view to making it a standard for reference, as well as to give an ample provision for general or special reading. . . . And the chief object of the collections—to present an array of good poetry so widely representative and so varied in its tone as to offer an answering chord to every mood and phase of human feeling—has been carefully kept in view, both in the selection and the arrangement of its contents. So that, in all senses, the realization of its significant title has been an objective point"—(Preface).

Useful for bibliography even though an older standard collection. Material is arranged topically. There is an alphabetical list of authors in the beginning of the volume and an alphabetical index of titles at the end.

"When the book appeared in 1870, it met with an instant and remarkably popular welcome, selling more than twenty thousand copies during the first six months"—(J. G. Wilson, MEMOIRS OF WILLIAM C. BRYANT).

CUNLIFFE, J. W. AND A. H. THORNDIKE.
Warner's Library of the World's Best Literature. New York: Warner Library Co., 1917. 30 vols.

First edited by Charles Dudley Warner, Hamilton Wright Mable, Brander Mathews, W. P. Trent and others, and re-issued in 1917 under the editorship of Cunliffe and Thorndike, this long famous literary encyclopedia-anthology has also appeared as the Columbia University Course in Literature, Based on the World's Best Literature.

The entries are arranged alphabetically by authors, movements, and source topics, providing for each author included a brief biographical sketch, followed by excerpts from his principal works. Biographical sketches are signed; references are made to the best available biography; and a list of important works by the author is indicated.

The general contents are as follows: volume one to twenty-six, an alphabetical arrangement of the world's best literature (sketches and selections); volume twenty-seven, songs and lyrics; volume twenty-eight, dictionary of authors; volume twenty-nine, digest of books; volume thirty, students course in literature, and a general index of authors, titles, subjects, national literature.

ELIOT, CHARLES W.
The Harvard Classics. New York: Collier, 1909. 50 vols.

The "Five Foot Shelf," as the collection is sometimes called, is a set of extracts from all those authors, ancient and modern, who have contributed to the cultural tradition of the Western World,—English, European, Greek, Latin, and Oriental. Selections vary in length from several pages to hundreds of pages and are representative of over seventy authors.

Volume 50 contains an analytical author, subject, and title index to all of the material contained in the set, and an index to the first lines of poems, songs, hymns, and psalms.

"This library seems truly to reflect the mind that assembled it. It is large, wise, serene, sure and contemplative. . . . We should imagine that the doctor's opinion about it is quite sound and true: that any man can have the essentials of a liberal education if he and these books become familiar friends"—(CURRENT OPINION, April, 1909).

"In its complete form it will inevitably illustrate the inability of individual taste, however cultivated, to prescribe a rigid course in the world's best literature which serves all readers" — (NEW YORK WORLD, April, 1909).

MACK, M. AND W. FROST AND L. DEAN.
English Masterpieces: An Anthology of Imaginative Literature from Chaucer to T. S. Eliot. New York: Prentice-Hall, 1950–1951. 8 vols.

Contents: Volume I, AGE OF CHAUCER; Volume II; ELIZABETHAN DRAMA; Volume III, RENAISSANCE POETRY; Volume IV, MILTON; Volume V, THE AUGUSTANS; Volume VI, ROMANTIC AND VICTORIAN POETRY; Volume VII, MODERN POETRY; Volume VIII, SELECTED PROSE.

MOULTON, CHARLES WELLS.
Library of Literary Criticism of English and American Authors. New York: Moulton Publishing Company, 1901–1905. 8 vols. Reprint issued in 1935–1940 by Peter Smith.

A compilation of fairly long extracts from reviews and criticisms of writings by important English and American Authors from 680 to 1904.

For each author included, there is given a brief biographical sketch and then selected quotations from criticisms of his work arranged as follows: (1) personal criticisms; (2) criticisms of individual works; (3) general criticisms. Volume eight contains two indexes: (1) authors criticized; (2) authors of the criticisms.

STEDMAN, E. C. AND E. M. HUTCHINSON.
Library of American Literature. New York: Charles L. Webster and Company, 1890. 11 vols.

Representative selections of the work of principal American Authors, 1607–1889, chronologically arranged according to authors. A biographical dictionary of the writers included is contained in volume eleven (pp. 467–614), as is also a general index of persons, subjects, and, in some instances, titles.

"This work . . . has increased in usefulness with each successive issue and now in its total of eleven large volumes opens as complete a survey of the history and character of the American mind as is possible by the method followed . . . a remarkable execution . . . soundness of judgment in selection . . . extraordinary breadth and variety of acquaintance with forgotten books and . . . impartiality and justice of . . . choice of authors"—(ATLANTIC, 66:707).

STEVENSON, BURTON E.

Home Book of Verse: American and English, 1580–1918. New York: Henry Holt and Company, 1915. 4009 p.

A collection of the familiar English and American poems from 1580–1922, with an appendix containing a few well-known poems in other languages, aiming, as the introduction states, to include nothing which did not seem to ring true; to recognize the validity of popular taste as well as of classical taste; to lay emphasis upon the lighter forms of verse; and to especially stress the work of living English and American poets, "particularly of the younger generation." Remarkable for its range and inclusiveness.

"Mr. Stevenson's selective power is shown perhaps to best advantage in his omissions, in his ability to remain unswayed by a more or less meretricious vogue. His striking and admirable discriminations against every influence that tends to impair the practice of poetry will appear upon examination of his work"—(THE NATION, November 9, 1918).

WINSLOW, OLA ELIZABETH.

Harper's Literary Museum. New York: Harper and Brothers, 1927.

The subtitle is: A Compendium of Instructive, Entertaining and Useful Matter Selected from Early American Writings Being the First of a Series of Volumes Covering Also Other Literatures and Times.

Since literary merit was not a principle of inclusion, preference, in fact, being evidenced for the odd, unfamiliar, and ordinary material, the work has definite usefulness for an understanding of the background of the times.

"A particularly amusing and revealing collection of American tidbits, including in a final section, representative advertisements from newspapers and handbills from the earliest time well on into the last century"—(THE NATION, January, 1927).

"The items that comprise it are in a large measure fresh discoveries, the arrangement modeled on that of the literary annual of the early 19th Century has a delightful miscellaneity of an old curio shop, and text and type both preserve in flavor the atmosphere of antiquity"—(NEW YORK HERALD TRIBUNE, January 28, 1927).

"The work of selecting and compiling the contents has been admirably done by Miss Winslow, for she has shown a notable discrimination in choosing extracts that are representative of the spirit of the time from which they are taken. The result is a volume especially colorful and flavory of ancient days"—(NEW YORK TIMES, December 11, 1927).

Histories of English Literature

BAUGH, ALBERT C. ED.
A Literary History of England. New York: Appleton-Century-Crofts, Inc., 1948.

A comprehensive history of the literature of England, scholarly and readable, suited to the needs of mature students of literature and to cultivated readers generally. The Old English section provides a noteworthy emphasis upon philological material; the Modern English section gives acceptable treatment to economics, politics, and sociology.

"One might carp and cavil endlessly about details of interpretation and emphasis . . . . but to do so would be to obscure the authors' positive achievement. They have not produced just another classroom textbook; they have furnished a comprehensive guide to their subject. . . . If the student or layman wants a particular piece of information, he may not always find it in this book. But if it isn't there, he can be fairly sure that the author will tell him precisely where to go next in his search"—(NEW YORK HERALD TRIBUNE, May 2, 1948).

"Since practically every writer of any importance is discussed, the references to each are necessarily brief, and sometimes, especially in the latter chapters, the judgments seem a little perfunctory. But all four sections are so crisply written that the book can be read for pleasure as well as for information"—(NEW YORKER, March 27, 1949).

GARNETT, R. AND E. GOSSE.

English Literature: An Illustrated Record. London: Heinemann; New York: Macmillan, 1903. 4 vols. Reprinted, 4 vols. in 2, 1935.

Aims to "stimulate and gratify curiosity concerning the leading authors of" England; to tell who the author was, what he looked like and wrote; "where he lived . . . what his handwriting was . . . and how he appeared in caricature to his contemporaries"—(Pref.)

The special reference value of the work resides in the many illustrations, largely derived from contemporary prints, illuminations, portraits, etc. The revised edition of 1923 adds a section on literature from 1902–1922. Beyond this, it does not differ from the original edition.

Referring to volume two a reviewer has noted: "While all the literature of this extraordinary period is reviewed with appreciative judgment, and as fully as the design of the work admits, most stress is naturally laid on those two great, and we might say mutually complementary, personages, Bacon and Shakespeare." Of volume four, the same reviewer wrote: "The writers of the last quarter of the eighteenth century and virtually the whole of the nineteenth will probably be to most readers the most attractive of all. . . . For the lives of these writers abundant details were at hand, and the editors have used them so as to seize the illuminating points." Of the complete work, the reviewer concluded: "it is a worthy history of the grandest body of literature in any modern language"—(THE NATION, March 3, 1904).

"The pictorial is the unique feature of this work, and it may be said at the outset that the publishers have amply fulfilled their promise to enforce this story of a nation's letters by a larger appeal to the eye than has ever before been attempted. . . . Mr. Garnett's scholarship has the calm, judicial comprehensiveness of the learned and the painstaking, but his language moves along with the lumbering dignity of an elephant." This history of literature is, "except for minor reservations . . . the most complete that has yet appeared, and as such it can justly claim to supersede its predecessors in the field of popular exposition"—(THE OUTLOOK, May 14, 1904).

WARD, A. W. AND A. R. WALLER.
Cambridge History of English Literature. London: Cambridge University Press, 1907–1927. 15 vols. A reprint, published in 1931 by Macmillan, lacks the bibliographies. The cheaper edition was also published by Cambridge in 1954.

An authoritative account of the successive movements of English literature, major and secondary. Each chapter is by a specialist and has a relatively full and useful bibliography. The bibliographies, the detailed index in the fifteenth volume, and the eminence of the contributors constitute the special features of the work. The standard book.

Among the representative reviews of the individual volumes of the work are the following:

Vol. I. "The volume has an interest as well as a value, only the interest is rather linguistic than literary"—(NEW YORK TIMES, December 28, 1907).

Vol. II. "To the reader of ordinary culture, the second volume seems vastly more interesting and instructive in the right sense, rather than the first volume"—(NEW YORK TIMES, June 20, 1908).

Vol. III. "The absence of any dominating names renders this volume even more useful for the student of English literature, since it is the second and third rate little masters about whom it is difficult to get full and accurate information such as is afforded in the present volume. Apart from a few defects the present volume seems to be fully up to the standard of the two preceding"—(NEW YORK TIMES, February 27, 1909).

"This rich composite history of English literature is a real service to English scholarship"—(SATURDAY REVIEW OF LITERATURE, May 1, 1909).

Vol. IV. "Taken as a whole, the volume is rather a disappointment; but it must be remembered that it is intended more as a book of reference than a readable and connected history of literature; and if this is borne in mind the present, as the preceding volumes, amply fulfills its purpose"—(NEW YORK TIMES, May 14, 1910).

Vols. V. & VI. "An admirable book of reference, but it is somewhat straining the use of words to call it a history of English literature. The bibliographical apparatus is on the same scale as in the previous volumes, and will probably form the useful portion of the whole series, though in the present section the work of Prof. Schelling has anticipated most of the special details"—(NEW YORK TIMES, January 29, 1911).

Vol. VIII. "The selection is remarkably comprehensive, and the arrangement is generally admirable. In general character the eighth volume possesses the scholarly sanity and thoroughness of its predecessors"—(NEW YORK TIMES, May 12, 1912).

"It was a happy thought to engage a leading authority on the Elizabethan Drama, like Professor Schelling, for this subject, inasmuch as one of the chief problems in the study of the Restoration Drama is its relation to that of the earlier years of the century . . .—(THE NATION, May 9, 1912).

Vol. IX. "If the greater portion of the present volume of the Cambridge history leaves much to be desired in the way of close characterization and philosophic grasp, it is, like its predecessors, an invaluable treasure house to the student of English literature"—(ATHENAEUM, December 20, 1913).

"The bibliographies make up about one-fourth of the entire volume, and in some sections have an exceptional value. For example, the list of Defoe's writings, compiled by Professor Trent, is the fullest and most accurate in existence"—(THE NATION, Feb. 27, 1913).

Vol. X. "We cannot conclude without offering those concerned our warmest congratulations on the bibliographies in this volume. They are marked by exceptional completeness and accuracy, and will be of the greatest value to students of the period"—(ATHENAEUM, November 21, 1913).

Vol. XI. "Taken as a whole, the volume quite sustains the high reputation of the series, while the value and bulk of the bibliographical studies at the end increases as modern times are approached"—(ATHENAEUM, November 21, 1914).

Vol. XII. "Some sixty pages are given to elaborate bibliographies, including an excellent one on the 'Relations of English and continental literatures in the romantic period" —(NEW YORK TIMES, March 5, 1916).

Vols. XIII. & XIV. "The chapters devoted to the literature of all the Dominions from the freshness of their matter and their treatment are among the most enthralling in the book"—(SATURDAY REVIEW OF LITERATURE, May 12, 1917).

"A grim and militant provincialism is the presiding spirit of the volumes. Only so can one explain the fact that Newman is mentioned only in scattered references and nowhere treated as the great master of prose that he was, that Meredith's MODERN LOVE is slurred over as unimportant, and that the treatment of Patmore's later verse ("The Toys," "Magna est veritas," etc.), of Henley, and of Pater is brief and grudging"—(DIAL, May 31, 1917).

"Mr. Robertson treats in too cursory and perfunctory a fashion the question of the historical value of Carlyle's works, nor does the bibliography supply the lacuna. . . ." —(ENGLISH HISTORICAL REVIEW, July, 1917).

WILSON, PERCY AND BONAMY DOBREE.

Oxford History of English Literature. London: Oxford University Press, 1945—.

When completed the work will consist of twelve volumes, covering the entire field of English literature from its earliest beginnings to the present. Each volume or partial volume will be an independent part of the series, written by an acknowledged authority and containing extensive bibliographies.

". . . . Now it is obvious enough that any literary history must discuss a great deal of work possessing little intrinsic merit, and that much of the historian's activity will necessarily be cultural sociology rather than criticism. But unless the primary concern is with that in literature which is alive for us as part of the "mind of Europe," the social and cultural history will lack power and significance. Unrelated to any clear system of value of judgments, it will tend to become a dull and academic recital of facts contributing nothing to the understanding of the relation between literary modes and ways of thinking and feeling, between quality of writing and quality of living. . . . It cannot be said that Mr. Bennett has altogether succeeded in avoiding this danger. . . .

". . . . In all fairness it must be said that there is little satisfying analysis of Chaucer to be found anywhere. . . .

". . . . As a whole the book is valuable chiefly as a scholarly summary of factual information. It cannot be said to have the same unity and organizing sections of Courthope's HISTORY OF ENGLISH POETRY"—(TIMES LITERARY SUPPLEMENT, April 17, 1948).

"Sir Edmund Chambers has here produced a most learned compendium of knowledge, but it is not among the most urbane and attractive of his great achievements, and even the scholar, apart from the mere student of literature may find the ample fare provided a little difficult to assimilate. . . .

"It is, no doubt, ungracious to ask for more when we have been given much, but it is . . . a matter for regret that Sir Edmund has not been given or has not taken the opportunity to write in the fulness of his wide scholarship a more complete account of English literature at the close of the Middle Ages"—(MODERN LANGUAGE REVIEW, XL 1).

". . . . Mr. Lewis's volume was certainly worth waiting for. Learned, vivacious, individual, this nine-years-pondered handbook is a notable performance.

"This book has so many virtues that we may be forgiven for calling attention to two particulars in which it is tiresome . . . giving his references, when he quotes, in the body of the text. . . . The other fault is a defective table of contents. . . . The same tiresomeness is found in the other volumes of the Oxford History"—(TIMES LITERARY SUPPLEMENT, September 17, 1954).

"Crammed as the book is, it is eminently readable. . . .

"One third of the whole book is occupied by Chronological Tables and an important . . . Bibliography under six headings covering the field with reasonable exhaustiveness. They give ample evidence of Professor Bush's accuracy and of his watchful eye for everything in print concerning his subject and his authors"—(MODERN LANGUAGE REVIEW, XL 1).

"Two difficulties which arise from Bush's method will occur to any reader, but they certainly cannot be called weaknesses of the book. The first is that in treating a topic such as "The Literature of France" the number of titles is so great and Bush's learning so imposing that the ordinary mortal will wish the eleven pages expanded into a monograph . . . a second difficulty inherent in the method of the volume is that the topical arrangement forces the historian to treat parts of the work of certain authors in one chapter and parts in other chapters" — (*Modern Language* QUARTERLY, IX).

Histories of American Literature

PARRINGTON, VERNON L.
Main Currents in American Thought. New York: Harcourt, Brace & Company, 1927–30. 2 vols.

A scholarly interpretation of American literature from the viewpoint of the main political and religious ideas that have influenced her from the beginning of her history. The first volume, THE COLONIAL MIND covers the period from 1620 to 1800; the second volume, THE ROMANTIC REVOLUTION IN AMERICA, covers the period, 1800 to 1860. Each volume contains an extensive bibliography.

"Technically the book is a piece of literary history. The evidence in the book is drawn largely from written sources; the influential American writings are individually considered with freshness and brilliance. But the treatment as a whole goes beyond most literary history" — (NEW YORK HERALD TRIBUNE, May 1, 1927).

QUINN, ARTHUR HOBSON.
The Literature of the American People: An Historical and Critical Survey. New York: Appleton-Century-Crofts, Inc., 1951.

A scholarly and readable treatment of literature, stressing its relation to the allied arts of painting, sculpture, architecture, politics, and social thought.

"Although it is obvious that no single book treating such a

vast subject can hope to please everyone, this one seems to fall short of what might be hoped for in the way of over-all organization and integration. . . . On the whole, and in spite of some of the faults suggested, the book is very competent and deserves wide use in the kind of courses for which it was prepared"—(UNITED STATES QUARTERLY BOOK REVIEW, Sept., 1951).

"Throughout the book there are many afterthoughts and many interpolations; the reader's attention is too often dragged from the consideration of development to the consideration of detail. . . . Many of the errors of detail and distortion of emphasis spring from an earnest patriotism which is prepared to twist all historical standards in order to create the illusion that literary progress in America has been constantly in alliance with the development of an American way of life . . . . chauvinism is seldom scholarly, and when chauvinism is designed for classroom reading, its fallacies take on proportions that are at times terrifying"—(LONDON TIMES, June 29, 1951).

SPILLER, R. E., W. THORP (and others).
Literary History of the United States. New York: The Macmillan Company, 1948. 3 vols.

The first two volumes constitute a survey of American literature from colonial times to the present. The third volume is a comprehensive bibliography. The chapters are not signed, but a list of the contributors is given in volume two (pp. 1393–1396).

"Nothing so good in the general presentation of American Literary History has yet appeared. Inclusive in scope, and judicious in its acumen, the history is a landmark and itself becomes a part of our growing tradition and an influence for the future. We have waited a long time for such a book; now that it has come, there can be nothing but gratification, congratulation and a sense of indebtedness to the group who are responsible for this highly significant work of criticism and scholarship"—(SATURDAY REVIEW OF LITERATURE, November 27, 1948).

". . . considers the development of American literature from both the critical and historical vantage point, and is written to read like a prolonged and freely flowing narrative"—(NEW YORKER, February, 1949).

"By banishing by-lines without going in for sufficiently sharp and unsparing editing, the designers of the LITERARY HISTORY have sacrificed what advantages there may be to a frank miscellany without achieving the impact of a homogeneous work"—(THE NATION, January 22, 1949).

". . . . But the treatment of specifically religious data in this survey does not seem to me to be on the same high level of competence with the rest of it. . . . There is room for someone to write a corresponding LITERARY HISTORY OF RELIGION IN THE UNITED STATES"—(CHRISTIAN CENTURY, Feb. 16, 1949).

"The new work is the result of careful planning, and it is in nearly every respect far better than the CAMBRIDGE HISTORY. . . . It is a book for which every serious student must be profoundly grateful; but it is not a definitive literary work and he who uses it should know its weaknesses as well as its strength"—(YALE REVIEW, Spring, 1949).

TRENT, W. P., J. ERSKINE (and others).
Cambridge History of American Literature. New York: Putnam, 1917–1921. 4 vols.

The 1954 reissue by Macmillan in three volumes is textually complete, but lacks the bibliographies (indexed in Northup's REGISTER) which are an important feature of the original edition.

Volume one covers colonial and revolutionary literature; volume two, early and later national literature; volumes three and four, later national literature. In its time, and perhaps at present, the most important history of American literature.

"A valuable, comprehensive, and from beginning to end, a more interesting book. Emphasis must be laid upon the care and detail which the authors and editors have devoted to the early literature of our land . . . . is of the utmost importance" —(NEW YORK TIMES, November 25, 1917).

"This history brings to our notice writers whom we should otherwise have overlooked; fills up gaps in our knowledge of the literary history of the country, and supplies accurate data as to the various activities of the press and the biographies of writers"—(SATURDAY REVIEW OF LITERATURE, May 31, 1919).

"On the whole, the history is a treasure house of information exhibited to the curious by intelligent guides. Not the least important part of these two volumes is the vast bibliographic index, covering 237 pages of small but clear types. Every important author has his detailed and dated list of works; and the word "important" is used generously. Then there is an immense list of critical books and articles invaluable to anyone who wishes to "work-up" an author or movement"—(NEW YORK TIMES, November 5, 1921).

". . . supersedes all earlier attempts to tell the story and appraise the achievement of our national literature"—(THE NATION, April 13, 1921).

"This lack of balance, together with the lack of contagious enthusiasm in the writing, and the dearth of comparative estimates constitute in our view faults which prevent us from extending such a cordial reception to the second volume as we did to the first"—(THE TIMES LITERARY SUPPLEMENT, July 17, 1919).

BIOGRAPHICAL DICTIONARIES

Indexes

Biography Index: A Cumulative Index to Biographical Material in Books and Magazines. New York: The H. W. Wilson Company, 1947—.

Appears quarterly (September, December and March), with annual cumulations in June. The first volume covers material published after January 1, 1946. The two sections of the index are: (1) Name alphabet, giving for each entry, full name, date, nationality, occupation; (2) Index by occupation.

"It includes current books in the English language wherever published; biographical material from the 1500 periodicals now regularly indexed in the Wilson indexes, plus a selected list of professional journals in the fields of law and medicine; obituaries of national and international interest from the NEW YORK TIMES. All types of biographical material are covered; pure biography, critical material of biographical significance, autobiography, letters, diaries, memoirs, journals, genealogies, fiction, drama, poetry, bibliographies, obituaries, pictorial works and juvenile literature. Works of collective biography are fully analyzed. Incidental biographical material such as prefaces and chapters in otherwise non-biographical books is included. Portraits are indicated when they appear in conjunction with indexed material . . ."—(Preface).

"It appears that the BIOGRAPHY INDEX will provide an up-to-date, well-organized service which should be valuable in all kinds of reference works"—(SUBSCRIPTION BOOKS BULLETIN, VOL. 18, NO. 2).

"The coverage of biographical material offered by this well-organized index is comprehensive and reliable. The BIOGRAPHY INDEX will be a useful and time-saving reference service for all types of libraries"—(SUBSCRIPTION BOOKS BULLETIN VOL. 18, NO. 4).

HEFLING, Helen and Eva Richards.
Index to Contemporary Biography and Criticism. New ed. rev. and enl. by Helen Hefling and Jessie W. Dyde . . . introd. by M. E. Hazeltine. Boston: Faxon, 1934. 229 p.

Supplements BIOGRAPHY INDEX for the period before 1936. The original work indexes some 200 collections of biography and criticism; the enlarged edition indexes 417 collections of biography and criticism. The alphabetical arrangement is by author and by title.

"It supplies a ready reference key to biography and criticism of figures important in the modern world—the word contemporary being defined as referring to persons whose birth occurred around the year 1850 or later. 417 book titles have been indexed in this edition, more than twice as many as for the first edition"—(WISCONSIN LIBRARY BULLETIN).

O'NEIL, Edward Hayes.
Biography by Americans, 1658–1936: A Subject Bibliography. Philadelphia: University of Pennsylvania Press; London: Milford, 1939. 465 p.

An alphabetical listing of all the known biographies authored by Americans. For the more famous men only the more important works are given. The arrangement is by biographical subject. Locates copies in eight libraries, but does not have an author index.

PHILLIPS, Lawrence Barnett.
Dictionary of Biographical Reference: Containing over 100,000 Names, Together with a Classed Index of the biographical literature of Europe and America. New ed. rev., cor. and augm. with supplements to date, by Frank Weitenkampf. Philadelphia: Gebbie, 1889. 1038 p.

Covers all periods; provides full name, identifying phrase, dates, and reference to collections containing biographical data.

RICHES, Phyllis.
Analytical Bibliography of Universal Collected Biography: Comprising Books Published in the English Tongue in Great Britain and Ireland, America and the British Dominions . . .

with an Introduction by Sir Frederic Kenyon. London: Library Association, 1934. 709 p.

Divided into three parts: (1) index of people written about, set up in an alphabetical order, following which are arranged short biographies alphabetically grouped by authors' names; (2) bibliography of the works dealt with, some evaluation of being supplied from standard bibliographies, while others are added by the compiler; (3) indexes, chronologically listed according to centuries and arranged alphabetically.

"It is one of those long needed works of reference which few would lightly undertake and fewer could have completed as efficiently as Miss Riches has completed this"—(TIMES LITERARY SUPPLEMENT, Dec. 6, 1934).

". . . . It is remarkable that she used neither the two sets of the Peabody Institute of Baltimore Catalog or the splendid Catalog of the Boston Athenaeum Library. . . . Some of the short titles, too, are misleading.

"Nevertheless, the work has been performed, seemingly, in a painstaking manner and deserves praise rather than blame. It surely fills a gap in our bibliographical handbooks and makes available many of out-of-the-way biographical treatments. As such it merits a place in every reference department in the country, for, in addition to its other values, it may well be used as a purchasing guide for libraries or bookstores"—(LIBRARY JOURNAL, July 15, 1935).

". . . but it might have been made more complete, accurate and up-to-date by checking such obvious sources as Minto's REFERENCE BOOKS, Mudge's GUIDE and the entry "Biographic Dictionaries" in the Subject Index of the London Library. These biographical dictionaries are not analyzed. . . .

"And so the book has its weaknesses, but it is a good book, and it has already proved its worth. All those who are interested in the problem which gives occasion to the book, and all those who make good use of it will be grateful to Miss Riches"—(LIBRARY QUARTERLY, January, 1936).

STAUFFER, DONALD ALFRED.

English Biography Before 1700. Massachusetts: Cambridge University Press, 1930.

Aims to consider historically and critically the art of biography from the earliest time to 1700. The principal purpose is to present new facts in the history of biography; the method is to give bibliographies of all the extant pieces of English biography and to describe the more important ones. The first part of the bibliography is a subject and author index of English biography before 1700.

The author "has a large sympathy with the men whose biographical efforts he interprets, and a quick eye for all their charm and their merit . . . The bibliography with which he concludes his work is a splendid example of what such a bibliography ought to be"—(SATURDAY REVIEW OF LITERATURE, November 29, 1930).

"The story which Dr. Stauffer tells with faithful weaving of a great many threads, thick and thin (and the whole guaranteed and much increased in value by some eighty pages of bibliography), is the growth of biography into recognition and practice as a literary art"—(TIMES LITERARY SUPPLEMENT, December 11, 1930).

STAUFFER, DONALD ALFRED.
The Art of Biography in 18th Century England: Bibliographical Supplement. Princeton, New Jersey: Princeton University Press, 1941. 293 p. 2 vols.

An attempt "to present as historically comprehensive a picture as possible of 18th Century biography.

Volume I: the initial parts of the chapters contain analytical discussions; the concluding parts are devoted to the most significant biographies, those that best illustrate the main positions of the chapter. Chapter VI considers individually the best-known biographies of the century.

Volume II: an alphabetical list of biographies read in connection with the study; descriptions of important biographies not taken up in the main text.

The pages of this work reveal "a microcosm, little mirrors of the times reflecting from a thousand facets the variety and vitality of life itself." However, the author "devotes many pages to discussing the social currents reflected in the biography of the period and the social forces that affected its development, without throwing any searching light upon them. . . . Professor Stauffer seizes upon the best critical comments of the eighteenth-century biographies, but he is less a critic himself

than a journalist-antiquary with a lively nose for news and an enjoyment of human nature"—(NEW REPUBLIC, May 26, 1931).

"Mr. Stauffer would have been better advised not to attempt to make such a big book. His material needs pruning and knitting more closely together. It would have been an additional advantage if the fortuitous element in the bibliography had been more decisively subordinated to the selective. The book bears everywhere the marks of enthusiasm and industry: it is unfortunately lacking in form"—(SPECTATOR, October 10, 1941).

"I feel strongly that this admirable book on English biography deserves to be ranked as a work of scholarship. . . . It would be an injustice to say that Mr. Stauffer has written a Baedeker's guide to his subject, although he is equally compendius. His book is altogether on a higher level. It has a good but unpretentious style, written with a gusto which unconsciously and most pleasantly reveals the author's genuine enthusiasm for letters. The writing of this book, one feels, was not a task but a pleasure"—(SATURDAY REVIEW OF LITERATURE, April 19, 1941).

International Dictionaries of Biography

Chamber's Biographical Dictionary: The Great of all Nations and all Times. Originally compiled by David Patrick and F. Hindes Groome. New ed., ed. by Wm. Geddie and J. L. Geddie. London: Chambers, 1949. 1006 p.

Brief sketches of over 10,000 of the most famous and notorious figures of all times and countries, Cleopatra to Eisenhower. Also contains an index of selected psuedonyms and nicknames (pp. 996–1006).

Current Biography: Who's News and Why. New York: The H. W. Wilson Company, 1940–.

A monthly publication, cumulated annually in a single alphabet and including all biographical sketches and obituary notices, featuring national and international names in the news of the day. The 1956 edition, the 17th annual cumulation with index,

1951–1956, includes biographies of 335 persons prominent in the news during 1956. Each issue generally provides: full name, pronunciation, dates of birth and death, occupation and reason for prominence, address, biographical sketch with portrait, and reference to further sources of information. Probably the most useful single source of biographical data on contemporary American and foreign persons of prominence.

HOEHN, MATTHEW.
Catholic Authors: Contemporary biographical sketches, 1930–1947. Newark, New Jersey: St. Mary's Abbey, 1952. 2 vols.

Aims simply to introduce the reader to contemporary Catholic writers. Does not attempt critical appraisal of the authors; affects no judgment of the catholicity of doctrine or thought.

Foreign authors are included if at least one of their works appears in translation. Of the 1,600 authors screened, 620 were selected. A Supplement, which bears a 1952 copyright, includes 374 additional entries.

"No really representative library, personal or institutional, is complete without CATHOLIC AUTHORS. . . . A prodigious and invaluable work"—(CATHOLIC WORLD, December, 1948).

"Father Hoehn can rest after a labor well done. It is a much-needed volume and arranged for the greater convenience of the majority of readers. . . . The author cannot hope to satisfy every conceivable taste or opinion. Suffice it to say that the selection of authors is good and that the biographical material is comprehensive and as up-to-date as could be expected in such a work.

"If you cannot find what you are looking for in these 620 biographies, it's either inconsequential or it doesn't exist"—(CATHOLIC WORLD, August, 1948).

HYAMSON, ALBERT M.
Dictionary of Universal Biography. New York: E. P. Dutton & Co., Inc., 1951. 679 p.

Supplies brief information (dates of birth and death, nationality, profession) of about 110,000 famous persons who died before 1950. Also indicates sources where further information is contained. The great change, an improvement I hope that will be received by all who consult the book is that every entry of this new edition contains an indication of the principal works of reference in which biographies of the subjects of the entries are found."

"One person, one line" the stated goal of the compiler, is generally achieved.

"A sampling of pages throughout the main section of the books reveals comparatively few entries where the date of death is later than 1930, and none later than 1947 were noted. There is, however, an Addenda of 86 names taken from the Annual Register 1948 and 1949. This edition features a Key to References, a list of twenty-four reference works in which full biographies of the subject can be found. . . . It is a scholarly, accurate work, compiled by an experienced editor".—(SUBSCRIPTION BOOKS BULLETIN, July, 1952).

International Who's Who. London: Europe Publications, 1935—.

An annual compilation of very brief biographies, often only three or four lines, of living internationally prominent persons of all countries. Especially valuable for the inclusion of representatives of smaller nations who are seldom cited elsewhere.

". . . aims to supplement and coordinate the national biographical reference books, not to supersede them. The editors are anonymous. According to the Forward, the editors have gone directly to the subjects themselves for their biographical data, as well as to the usual sources . . . omitting but few biographies of international significance in the fields they have sought to cover, namely, economics, banking, minerology, diplomacy, music, authorship, art, science, criminology, science, history, medicine, industry, law, education, the judiciary, anthropology, the church, insurance, and sociology"—(SUBSCRIPTION BOOKS BULLETIN, 1948).

"Much work has been put into it, and to secure accuracy a questionnaire has been sent to the hundreds of people whose names appear. The value of the work consists in the fact that although many, perhaps most, of the names can be found in the national Who's Who, the task of searching innumerable volumes in many languages is quite impossible to all but a few"—(MANCHESTER GUARDIAN, December, 1936).

KUNITZ, Stanley J.
Living Authors: A Book of Biographies. New York: H. W. Wilson Company, 1931. 466 p.

Concise and very readable biographical sketches of 371 living authors of many different nationalities, with portraits and brief lists of their principal works. As stated in the WILSON BULLETIN, these are "lively and unconventional in tone but frequently useful for estimates and biographical data, not easily found elsewhere."

"Many of the writers are so recently arrived at fame . . . that they will not be found in any other work of reference. . . . The descriptions are catholic, and there seems to be few notable exceptions from contemporary eminence.

". . . . The defect of the compilation is its desire to be an entertainment as well as a work of reference. . . . Yet the book is better than its tone might imply"—(TIMES LITERARY SUPPLEMENT, August 13, 1931).

"This compilation may be called a new and useful kind of reference book, interesting enough for casual conning . . . equally well-planned for what we believe to be a more general though lower-browed comment in the personalities of public performers"—(BOSTON TRANSCRIPT, June, 1931).

"Whatever other reference book you have, you can still use this"—(SATURDAY REVIEW OF LITERATURE, July 27, 1931).

"A volume for days of pleasant browsing, as well as for the perennial reference shelf"—(CATHOLIC WORLD, September, 1931).

KUNITZ, Stanley J.
Authors Today and Yesterday. New York: H. W. Wilson Co., 1933.

Brief and readable biographical sketches of 320 authors whose works appeared mainly since 1900. The biographies in the companion volume, LIVING AUTHORS, are not repeated, but a Joint Index to biographies in both volumes is contained in AUTHORS TODAY AND YESTERDAY.

Generally speaking, the biographies in this volume are about twice the length of those in the earlier work; the number of foreign authors is larger.

"Many of the writers have contributed short autobiographies and others have supplied information. Each of the biographies is accompanied by a portrait and bibliography. To a person interested in contemporary and recent literature, the book is fascinating"—(COMMONWEAL, Feb. 23, 1934).

"Either one of these two books is useful and fascinating alone. Together they form a lively dictionary of contemporary literary biography"—(NEW YORK TIMES, March 11, 1934).

"An effective supplement to LIVING AUTHORS. . . . Together, the two books provide a convenient and fairly complete library of general information about contemporary writers"—(NEW REPUBLIC, April 11, 1934).

KUNITZ, STANLEY J. AND H. HAYCRAFT.
Twentieth Century Authors: A Biographical Dictionary of Modern Literature, Complete in One Volume with 1850 biographies and 1700 portraits. New York: The H. W. Wilson Co., 1942. 1577 p.

Differs somewhat from the earlier volumes in offering critical comment. As the authors state in the Preface, the "editorial policy in offering a descriptive comment has not been to attempt an independent appraisal, but to give a few summations of reliable critical comments."

The 1955 edition, TWENTIETH CENTURY AUTHORS: First Supplement, edited by Stanley J. Kunitz, assisted by Vineta Colby, "brings the original biographies and bibliographies up-to-date and contains some 700 new biographies, 670 with portraits, mostly of authors who have come into prominence since 1942, though with the inclusion of a small number of older authors whose omission from the earlier volumes it has seemed advisable to rectify. The total listing of approximately 2,550 names is to be found . . . incorporated into a single alphabet"—

"It kept us waiting four years and is worth it. . . . LIVING AUTHORS set a standard back in 1931; AUTHORS TODAY AND YESTERDAY maintained it; this surpasses them both"—(BOOKS, January 24, 1943).

"Invaluable for reference libraries, interesting to everyone who wishes to be informed about the person behind the book he reads"—(CHRISTIAN SCIENCE MONITOR, March 13, 1943).

". . . an indispensable tool for any library that boasts even a modest reference department. It will also prove invaluable to anyone with a modicum of curiosity concerning the men and women who have done, or are doing, the imaginative and non-imaginative writing of our times.

". . . more than doubles the usefulness of the earlier books. "The editors have been generous in their conception of what authorship in the twentieth century means"—(LIBRARY QUARTERLY, October, 1943).

ROMIG, WALTER.
Book of Catholic Authors: Informal self-portraits of famous modern Catholic writers, with preface and notes.

Some fifty sketches of "famous modern Catholic writers,—poets, essayists, novelists, sociologists, historians, editors, and lecturers, with portraits and a list of the author's writings.

"It is of course far from complete, but we are promised a second and third series if this first volume receives a hearty welcome. We are confident that it will"—(CATHOLIC WORLD, January, 1943).

SHARP, ROBERT F.
Short Biographical Dictionary of Foreign Literature. New York: Dutton, 1933. 302 p.

A concise biographical dictionary of some 550 authors, with short biographical notes and a list as practicable as possible of first editions of author's works. "Where an English translation of a work exists, the title of the translation is inserted after that of the original."

THOMAS, JOSEPH.
Universal Pronouncing Dictionary of Biography and Mythology. Philadelphia: Lippincott, 1930. 1550 p.

More popularly known as LIPPINCOTT'S BIOGRAPHICAL DICTIONARY, this work has long been a standard reference source and, though now long out of print (the 1930 printing being actually the third edition of the 1901 edition, revised and brought up to date), is still very useful as a ready reference. Includes persons of all nations and times, and names from many mythologies,

—Greek, Roman, Teutonic, Sanskrit, and others. Some articles are fairly long, but most are quite brief.

The Appendixes comprise: (1) Vocabulary of Christian (or first) names, with pronunciations and equivalents in the principal foreign languages; (2) Disputed or doubtful pronunciations.

Webster's Biographical Dictionary: A Dictionary of Names of Noteworthy Persons, with Pronunciations and Concise Biographies. Springfield, Massachusetts: G. & C. Merriam Company, 1943. 1697 p.

Contains approximately 40,000 entries, not restricted by period, nationality, race, religion, or occupation, about one-third of which are of living men and women. The sketches are generally at least several lines in length, often reaching twenty lines, and not infrequently forty lines or more. Among the special features are: the effort which is made to give syllabic division and pronunciation of all names; the tables of United States presidents, vice-presidents, justices of the Supreme Court, and sovereigns of foreign nations.

Although the entries are unsigned, and one must still resort to such monumental biographical dictionaries as the DNB and the DAB for more extended treatment and for critical evaluation, the facts given in this work for each person are generally trustworthy and sufficiently full for the great majority of inquirers.

"The nineteen pages of "A Guide to Pronunciation" of words in each of the languages concerned is a marvel of composition and clarity for so complex a subject. William Allen Deilson . . . and . . . staff . . . deserve our thanks for producing such a handy, volume"—(LIBRARY JOURNAL, 69:1944, 164).

"The biographies are competent, succinct and remarkably informative for the space they cover"—(THE COMMONWEAL, October 29, 1943).

"Particular pains have been taken with respect to the correct pronunciation and syllabic division of the names; and for this information, as well as for the dates and other main facts concerning the persons included, the volume is an invaluable reference tool"—(LIBRARY QUARTERLY, January, 1944).

"The style . . . is concise and condensed, but clear and

comprehensive. . . . The format of the book is exceptionally good. . . . Recommended"—(SUBSCRIPTION BOOKS BULLETIN, July, 1944).

Who's Who Among Living Authors of Older Nations: Covering the Literary Activities of Living Authors and Writers of All Countries of the World except the United States of America, Canada, Mexico, Alaska, Hawaii, Newfoundland, the Philippines, the West Indies and Central America. Vol. 1, 1931–32, ed. by A. Lawrence. Los Angeles, California: Golden Syndicate Publishing Co., 1932. 482 p.

Three principal sections: (1) an alphabetical arrangement of authors; (2) a press section comprising biographies of editors, magazine and press writers, with names of periodicals in which their writings appear; (3) supplement, containing a list of authors and writers by countries, a list of poets by countries, a list of authors showing pen names, a list of pen names showing real names.

"Recommended for the library able to afford this somewhat expensive addition to its reference resources"—(SUBSCRIPTION BOOKS BULLETIN, July, 1932).

World Biography. New York: Institute for Research in Biography, Inc., 1940.

The first three editions appeared as: BIOGRAPHICAL ENCYCLOPEDIA OF THE WORLD. The fourth edition, which appeared in 1948 in two volumes (5,120 p.), contains about 40,000 "who's who" type sketches of important living persons of over sixty nations of the world. The fifth edition appeared in 1954.

". . . there are twice as many names in WORLD BIOGRAPHY as in any other international work, and the proportion is even greater. WORLD BIOGRAPHY is a very useful library tool"—(SUBSCRIPTION BOOKS BULLETIN, April, 1949).

English Biographical Dictionaries

BOASE, FREDERICK.
Modern English Biography: Containing Many Thousand Concise Memoirs of Persons Who Have Died Since 1950, with an

Index of the Most Interesting Matter. Truro: Netherton, 1892–1921. 6 vols.

Aims to give the essential facts of each life and, in the case of authors, brief but accurate titles of their principal work and references to books where longer accounts may be found. Especially useful for minor nineteenth century names not included in the DNB. The first three volumes (A-Z, Index) appeared between 1892–1901; the last three (suppl. vols. 1–3, A-Z) appeared between 1908–1921. Contains a useful subject index, providing lists of pseudonyms, fancy names, class lists, et cetera.

". . . there is no service which any serious student can rank higher than that of the good guide who will prevent waste of precious time by giving what we may call basic facts, and offering the first clues for further study"—(NOTES AND QUERIES, November 5, 1921).

". . . most valuable work of reference"—(ATHENAEUM, August 14, 1897).

Catholic Who's Who. London: Burns, Oates & Washburne, Ltd. 1908—.

Originally published as an annual, the title until 1935 being CATHOLIC WHO'S WHO AND YEARBOOK, the 34th edition appeared in 1941, the 35th edition, in 1952.

"After eleven years the CATHOLIC WHO'S WHO has again come out. It contains 5,500 biographies of Catholics in Great Britain, the Commonwealth and Ireland, and 'is the most substantial book of reference about Catholic personalities, ecclesiastical and lay, in the language.'

"It has been well edited and does not, as used to be the case, concentrate mainly on the aristocracy and the government services. The arts are excellently represented"—(AMERICA, August 9, 1952).

"For all who are engaged in Catholic (or indeed any) journalism, publishing or bookselling, this is a reference book of immense value which will save hours of valuable time; all reference libraries will want a copy"—(BOOKS ON TRIAL, June, 1952).

KUNITZ, S. J. AND H. HAYCRAFT.
British Authors Before 1800: A Biographical Dictionary. New York: The H. W. Wilson Company, 1952. 584 p.

Contains 650 biographies and 220 portraits of English authors, major and minor, from the dawn of English literature to Cowper and Burns. The sketches, which range in length from 300 to 1,500 words—roughly proportionate to the importance of the subject—are followed by a list of the principal works of the biographee, with dates of the original publication and selected source material.

"The information is attractively presented and is generally correct and abreast of current scholarly research. As a reference work it seems to be directed to the beginning student or to the general reader and to be designed for the small library which does not possess the DICTIONARY OF NATIONAL BIOGRAPHY, the CAMBRIDGE BIBLIOGRAPHY OF ENGLISH LITERATURE, or the BRITANNICA—although in several instances it corrects information in some of these standard sources. . . . When the editors have checked with modern scholarly research, their summaries are accurate and informed (e.g., Boswell and Pope). When they have omitted to do so, they perpetuate old errors"—(LIBRARY QUARTERLY, October, 1953).

". . . brief, careful, factual reporting characterizes the sketches of the book . . . but one wonders about a decision to include Mary Godwin and not William"—(SATURDAY REVIEW OF LITERATURE, March 21, 1953).

"This latest volume of the Wilson 'author books' will be welcomed for every reference collection"—(WISCONSIN LIBRARY BULLETIN, November, 1952).

KUNITZ, S. J. AND H. HAYCRAFT.
British Authors of the Nineteenth Century. New York: The H. W. Wilson Company, 1936. 677 p.

Contains some 1,000 biographies and 350 portraits of the nonliving major and minor British authors of the nineteenth century. The sketches, which range in length from 100 to 2,500 words, depending upon the importance of the subject, are followed by a list of the principal works of the author, with dates of the original publication and selected source material.

". . . the salient facts . . . are so chosen and pointed that the men and women presented emerge as personalities, products of their ancestry, impressed by their times and leaving their own impress on those times in turn. . . . Some of the Catholic sketches—for example, that of Lord Acton—are guilty of wrong emphasis"—(COMMONWEAL, January 15, 1937).

"Students of English literature who have had to get their information about authors' lives from the usual encyclopedias of biography with their bone-dry listings of dates and titles will be grateful for the book. . . . Not only are the characterizations more than ordinarily vivid; the literary quality of the various sketches is well above the average to be found in such collections; the book should be widely used"—(NEW REPUBLIC, January 27, 1937).

"An invaluable reference book. Contains brief but competent biographies of at least 1,000 persons . . . should prove indispensable to all those whose work or interest demands information on writers"—(SATURDAY REVIEW OF LITERATURE, December 19, 1936).

Dictionary of National Biography. Leslie Stephen and Sir Sidney Lee, eds. London: Smith, Elder, and Company and Oxford University Press, 1885—.

The most complete and the most authoritative work of its kind, containing more than 30,000 biographies of deceased Britons. First published in 63 volumes, it was reissued in 22 volumes in 1908–1909, the 22nd volume being the supplement of persons who had been omitted in the first selection either because they were still alive at the time or because their importance had been originally underestimated. The second supplement (ed. Sir Sidney Lee) added 1,660 articles about individuals who died up to January 1, 1912. The third supplement (eds. H. W. C. Davis and J. R. H. Weaver) covered the period 1912 to 1921. The fourth supplement (ed. L. G. W. Weaver) covered the period 1922 to 1930 and contained an Index covering all supplements 1901–1930. The fifth supplement (ed. L. G. W. Legg) covered the period 1931 to 1940 and contained an Index covering all supplements 1901–1940. THE CONCISE DICTIONARY OF NATIONAL BIOGRAPHY is an epitome volume which lists all the persons included in the foundation work and its supplements. The articles, however, are reduced to about one fourteenth of the original work.

The foundation work, its supplements, and the concise D.N.B. include biographies of virtually every prominent

Briton whose life-period falls within the date-lines of D.N.B. publications.

"A competent and representational review of the greats of England. A must for every well-organized library. The D.N.B. is unsurpassed for all-around balance and or authority. Recommended"—(SUBSCRIPTION BOOKS BULLETIN, April, 1932).

"The language of commendation becomes almost monotonous in dealing with the successive volumes of the Dictionary of National Biography"—(LONDON TIMES, October 2, 1891).

Who's Who: An Annual Biographical Dictionary, with which is Incorporated Men and Women of the Time. New York: Macmillan, 1849—.

An annual publication—the pioneer work of its kind—giving brief biographical facts about living men and women and, in the case of writers, a chronological list of publications. Principally British, but not completely so, since it also includes a number of internationally famous names (e.g., Franklin Delano Roosevelt, Mussolini, Hitler, Stalin).

The content order of the typical WHO'S WHO is generally: (1) A list of abbreviations; (2) Obituary; (3) The Royal Family, with portraits, all in the preliminary pages spaced between advertisements; (4) Biographies, in alphabetical order, with each sketch containing full names, degrees, honors, present position, birth, parents' names, education, publications, present address.

WHO'S WHO is supplemented by editions of WHO WAS WHO, which contains the biographies of those who died during the period. Each volume contains the final biographical sketches of deceased persons previously listed in WHO'S WHO, generally only with the date of death added,—in a few instances, with some additional information.

"Because of the scope and accuracy and because it continues to be the standard reference tool of its type in the British market, WHO'S WHO is highly recommended"—(SUBSCRIPTION BOOKS BULLETIN, April, 1950).

American Biographical Dictionaries

American Catholic Who's Who. Detroit, Michigan: Walter Romig, 1934—.

An earlier edition, published by B. Herder in St. Louis, 1911, was edited by G. P. Curtis. Short biographical sketches of outstanding American Catholic churchmen and persons prominent in all fields and professions.

Appleton's Cyclopedia of American Biography. J. G. Wilson and John Fiske, eds. New York: D. G. Appleton & Company, 1887–1900. 7 vols.

Fairly long biographical sketches of the native and adopted citizens of the United States; as well as of eminent individuals of Canada, Mexico, and other countries of North and South America; and persons of foreign birth closely connected with American history. Contains many portraits, facsimiles of autographs, but little bibliography.

Contains, according to several sources, many utterly fictitious biographies; yet the accuracy rating of its other entries is said to be impressive. Practically superseded by the DAB, but still useful for names and information (e.g., illustrations, facsimiles of autographs), not included in the later work.

The edition entitled CYCLOPEDIA OF AMERICAN BIOGRAPHY (New York Press Association Compilers, Inc.), published in 1915, represents a slight revision of the Appleton. Six nonalphabetical supplementary volumes (VII–XII) were released by the same publisher between 1918 and 1931.

Dictionary of American Biography. Allen Johnson, ed. New York: Charles Scribner's Sons. 1928–1937. 21 vols. (Revised edition with Index and Supplement 1, 1943–45, 22 vols.)

Dictionary of American Biography. Published under the Auspices of the American Council of Learned Societies. Supplement 2, Robert Livingston Schuyler, ed.; Edward T. James, assoc. ed. New York: Scribner, 1958. 745 p.

Supplement 1 is volume 21 of the main work. Supplement 2, volume 22, contains 585 biographies of persons who died during the period 1936–40 inclusive, and follows the general pattern of the basic volumes.

The title-page verso of each volume contains the following statement: "Prompted solely by a desire for public service the New York Times Company and its President, Mr. Adolph S.

Ochs, have made possible the preparation of the manuscript of the DICTIONARY OF AMERICAN BIOGRAPHY through a subvention of more than $500.000 and with the understanding that the entire responsibility for the contents of the volumes rests with the American Council of Learned Societies."

Incorporates three restrictions in the definition of "American biography": (1) no living persons; (2) no persons who had not lived in the territory now known as the United States; (3) no British officer serving in America after the Colonies had declared their independence.

Although the DAB is narrower in scope than APPLETON'S CYCLOPEDIA OF AMERICAN BIOGRAPHY, which includes Canadian and Latin-American names, and is less inclusive than the NATIONAL CYCLOPAEDIA OF AMERICAN BIOGRAPHY, which includes many more minor names, it possesses more distinctive articles than either and far better bibliographies. The biographies range in length from 500 to 16,000 words, depending upon the importance of the subject.

"A most excellent biographical encyclopedia. . . . The accounts are fresh and from first hand sources. . . . Recommended"—(SUBSCRIPTION BOOKS BULLETIN, January 27, 1931).

"No such dictionary can be perfect, and this one has its defects; but it attains a level of excellence that will delight its users and make it of comprehensive and permanent value. It is bound to prove a fertilizing agency in historical and biographical work of every kind. This first volume promises also a wealth of curious and important lore which will inevitably be utilized as a starting point, broadened, and applied in a hundred different fields"—(SATURDAY REVIEW OF LITERATURE, January 12, 1929).

An overwhelming work; "careful reading of these volumes will greatly enrich the knowledge of even the more erudite scholar"—(AMERICAN HISTORICAL REVIEW, October, 1929).

KUNITZ, S. J. AND H. HAYCRAFT.
American Authors, 1600–1900: A Biographical Dictionary of American Literature, Complete in one Volume with 1300 biographies, 400 portraits. New York: The H. W. Wilson Company, 1938. 846 p.

Includes major and minor authors who contributed to the making of our literary history from the time of the first English settlement in Jamestown in 1607 to the close of the nineteenth century. Excludes living authors. The sketches, which range from 150 to 250 words, roughly proportionate to the importance of the subject, are followed by a list of the printed works of the biographee, original dates of publication, and a list of biographical and critical sources.

". . . in spite of occasional straining for freshness, the compilation has literary merit and the virtue of inclusiveness"—(BOOK REVIEW DIGEST, 1939).

". . . an invaluable reference book for literary students, librarians, writers, and just plain readers"—(NEW YORKER, October 29, 1938).

Lamb's Biographical Dictionary of the United States. J. H. Brown, ed. Boston: Federal Book Company, 1900–1903. 7 vols.

An alphabetical arrangement of short sketches. Useful because of the inclusion of some names not found in APPLETON'S CYCLOPAEDIA OF AMERICAN BIOGRAPHY or in the NATIONAL CYCLOPAEDIA OF AMERICAN BIOGRAPHY.

Also published in ten volumes by the Biographical Society (Boston, 1904) as TWENTIETH CENTURY BIOGRAPHICAL DICTIONARY OF NOTABLE AMERICANS (Rossiter Johnson, ed.).

National Cyclopaedia of American Biography. New York: James T. White & Company, Inc., 1892–. 41 vols.

Biographical sketches of all persons who are prominently connected with the history of the nation,—rulers, statesmen, soldiers, clergymen, lawyers, artists, literary men, scientists, representatives of professions generally, and even those who have contributed to the industrial and commercial progress and growth of the country. The arrangement is by period, field or profession, and by reference to important events or movements. An Index at the end of each volume lists alphabetically: (1) biographies of persons included; (2) general categories under which the names are arranged, with cross-indexing to the names connected with the categories. More comprehensive than the DAB; more current than APPLETON'S or LAMB'S.

Supplementary volumes keep the NATIONAL current, and all

volumes are indexed in a special locked binder, which is divided into three parts: I, volumes 1–30; II, volumes 31–41 (present permanent volume); III, current volumes.

Of volumes I–XX, a reviewer noted: "The current volumes are useful. Biographies of men and women living at the time the volumes were issued are included and the material is valuable because these men are important enough to have their biographies used frequently but not sufficiently important to have the material accessible elsewhere. . . . The current volumes only are recommended as useful in large reference collections"—(SUBSCRIPTION BOOKS BULLETIN, January, 1918).

"Like the earlier volumes, they include information on some persons about whom little or nothing else is available in most libraries. At the same time, much of this material is not likely to be ofen needed, except where there is local interest in certain individuals. Volumes XXI–XXVI are recommended as an auxiliary source for American biography in libraries with large reference collections"—(SUBSCRIPTION BOOKS BULLETIN, April, 1938).

PRESTON, WHEELER.

American Biographies. New York and London: Harper, 1940. 1147 p.

Very brief sketches, two or three item bibliographies, of names which are virtually all found more fully treated in the DAB; hence mainly of value in the small library which lacks the larger work.

"The rather short sketches emphasize accomplishment rather than details of personal life and are briskly concise and informative. A special feature is the bibliography supplied for further reference under every name"—(NEW YORK TIMES, November 10, 1940).

"More than 5,000 compact biographical sketches of Americans, from Colonial times to the present. The names of living people have been expressly omitted . . . with this exception, every man or woman from Colonial times onward who has played a noteworthy part in the making of the United States finds a place . . . including non-Americans who had a share in the history of the nation"—(BOOKLIST, December 15, 1940).

White's Conspectus of American Biography: A Tabulated Record of American History and Biography. 2d ed. New York: James T. White & Company, Inc., 1937. 455 p.

A revision and modernization of A CONSPECTUS OF AMERICAN BIOGRAPHY, which was published in 1906 in combination with the indexes to the NATIONAL CYCLOPAEDIA OF AMERICAN BIOGRAPHY. Useful both as a classified index to the NATIONAL CYCLOPAEDIA and as an independent tool of information.

"The chief merit of this work is that it affords a chronological survey of Americans active in government affairs, letters, and the arts. It is possible to learn from these lists at once who were Presidents, vice-presidents, cabinet officers, senators, congressmen, American ministers and ambassadors, heads of bureaus, governors, and chief justices of the states in any year since the establishment of the governmental unit concerned"—(SPRINGFIELD REPUBLICAN, April 11, 1938).

"Though part of the matter which makes up WHITE'S CONSPECTUS is available in almanacs or other volumes found in most libraries, some of it is not so easily located. It is brought together here in a convenient form which makes it, in spite of certain flaws, useful for quick reference. The CONSPECTUS is recommended for large libraries and also for smaller libraries whose need for this type of material might justify the expenditure"—(SUBSCRIPTION BOOKS BULLETIN, April 1938).

Who's Who in America: A Biographical Dictionary of Notable Living Men and Women. Chicago: The A. N. Marquis Company, 1949—.

The best known and the most generally useful dictionary of contemporary biography. Aims to include the names of the best known men and women in all lines of useful and reputable achievement. The standards of admission are: "(1) those selected on account of special prominence in creditable lines of effort making them subjects of extensive interest, inquiry or discussion; and (2) those included arbitrarily on account of position—civil, military, educational, corporate or organizational."

For those who are not listed in WHO'S WHO IN AMERICA, or for whom additional information is desired, one should refer to the more specialized dictionaries of the "WHO'S WHO" type: local (e.g., WHO'S WHO IN THE MIDWEST); professional (e.g., WHO'S WHO IN COMMERCE AND INDUSTRY); foreign-American (e.g., WHO'S WHO IN POLISH AMERICA); religious or social (WHO'S WHO IN AMERICAN JEWRY).

"It is the standard reference work in its field and has no serious competitors . . . Because of its accuracy, breadth of scope, and general reference utility, it is a recommended reference work" — (SUBSCRIPTION BOOKS BULLETIN, July, 1950).

WILLARD, F. AND M. LIVERMORE.
A Woman of the Century: 1470 Biographical sketches accompanied by portraits of leading American women in all walks of life.

A useful supplement insofar as it contains sketches of important women of the nineteenth century whose biographies appear in no other reference work.

INDEXES

To Indexes

HASKELL, DANIEL C.
A Checklist of Cumulative Indexes to Individual Periodicals in the New York Public Library. New York: Library, 1942. 1946 p.

An alphabetical list of thousands of cumulative indexes available in the New York Public Library.

IRELAND, NORMA OLIN.
An Index to Indexes: A Subject Bibliography of Published Indexes. Boston: Faxon, 1942. 107 p.

Aims to assemble into one volume a selection of published indexes which will aid librarians, students, and scholars who need to locate quickly the index source of various subject fields. Characteristically, five types of indexes are used: (1) Special Indexes; (2) Indexes to sets of books; (3) Periodical Indexes; (4) Cumulative indexes to individual periodicals; (5) Government document indexes. Embraces 1,000 separate indexes listed under 280 different subjects.

"The book is neither comprehensive nor consistent, and it does not bring all the indexes mentioned down to date"—(AMERICAN HISTORICAL REVIEW, January, 1943).

"Mrs. Ireland by her broad and somewhat loose definition of 'index' permits the inclusion of indexes to periodicals, documents, and books, bibliographies, and check lists, and related publications. It is obvious that she had to limit herself to a selection. Foreign indexes are A PRIORI excluded. The result is somewhat discouraging"—(LIBRARY JOURNAL, March, 1943).

IRELAND, NORMA OLIN.
Local Indexes in American Libraries: A Union List of Unpublished Indexes. Boston: Faxon, 1947. 221 p.

A companion to Ireland's AN INDEX TO INDEXES.

To Ephemeral Materials

Vertical File Index. New York: The H. W. Wilson Company, 1935–. 640 p.

Formerly called, THE VERTICAL FILE SERVICE CATALOG; this publication is issued every month (except August), with an annual cumulation in December, and, for material listed, provides title, author, paging, publisher, and price.

"An annotated subject list of pamphlets, booklets, brochures, leaflets, circulars, folders, maps, posters, charts, mimeographed bulletins and other inexpensive material which falls outside the classification of books, but still has a place in the library . . . Some of the pamphlets are frankly propaganda or advertising, often biased in viewpoint but, like the other titles in the catalogue, they are listed in the belief that they may prove to be of some reference value"–(Preface).

To Newspapers and Serials

AYER, N. W. AND SONS.
Directory of Newspapers and Periodicals: Guide to Publications Printed in the United States and its Possessions, the Dominion of Canada, Bermuda, Cuba and Republic of the Philippines; Descriptions of the States, Provinces, Cities and Towns in which They Are Published; Classified Lists; 70 Maps. Philadelphia: Ayer, 1880–.

The stated purpose of the work is, "to provide, first, facts about those publications that are essential in the promotion of commercial and other interests through advertising." Hence the primary reference value of Ayer's is for current information about newspapers and periodicals such as: names of publishers and editors; frequency of publications; special leanings and interests; format; price and circulations. It is also useful for information of a geographical nature, such as: location, population, chief industries, distances to places of importance. "The standard list."

New York Daily Tribune Index, 1875–1906. New York: Tribune Association, 1876–1907. 31 vols.

More limited in scope than the NEW YORK TIMES INDEX, but still useful for the period covered. No longer published.

New York Times Index, 1913–. New York: New York Times Index, 1913–.

Appeared as a quarterly until 1929; as a monthly until 1948; as a semimonthly, with a cumulative annual, since 1948. It is today also available in microfilm. The scope of this carefully constructed work is evident from a description of the 1949 issue which contains 20,000 personal names separately indexed; 18,000 additional names of institutions and associations; 940 geographical headings; 175 listings of educational institutions; and 3,500 more subjects given under separate headings.

"Besides being primarily an index to the NEW YORK TIMES, the INDEX is also an independent reference work in that the entries give a synopsis of the newspaper articles. It serves as a guide to the publication of news in other newspapers"—(PUBLISHERS WEEKLY, 158:671, August 12, 1950).

Palmer's Index to the Times Newspaper, 1790–. Palmer's Index to the TIMES Newspaper, 1790–. London: Palmer, 1868–.

Considerably briefer than the official index of the TIMES of London, but still useful because of the length of time covered. "The indexing of obituary, death and funeral notices under the heading "Deaths" in each volume frequently supplies biographical material difficult to find elsewhere."

SEVERANCE, HENRY O.

A Guide to the Current Periodicals and Series of the United States and Canada. Michigan: Michigan University Press, 1931.

The first edition appeared in 1907; the second, in 1909; the third, in 1913; the fourth, in 1920; the fifth, in 1931. Includes fewer titles than the AYER AND SONS DIRECTORY, but is handier and more convenient mainly because of its alphabetical arrangement.

". . . an accessible and reliable source of information regarding American periodicals, society publications, and society transactions"—(THE LIBRARY JOURNAL, July, 1907, 334–335).

Times Official Index, 1906–. London: Times Office, 1907–.

A valuable reference tool; contains a detailed alphabetical index referring to date, page, and column. Originally published as a monthly, with annual cumulations for 1906–1913, it has been published, since 1914, in quarterly cumulations.

Ulrich's Periodical Directory: A Classified Guide to a Selected List of Current Periodicals, Foreign and Domestic. 8th ed. New York: R. R. Bowker Company, 1956. 740 p.

The first edition appeared in 1932; the second, in 1935; the third, in 1938; the fourth, in 1943; the fifth, in 1947; the sixth, in 1951; the seventh, in 1953; the eighth, in 1956. Different editions have special features. Thus the fourth edition was an Inter-American edition, covering North, Central, and South America, the West Indies, and Hawaii; the fifth edition emphasized the publications of North and South America and the British Empire; the sixth edition includes many foreign titles which were left out during the war years.

More than 7,500 periodicals are included in the various entries which include title, subtitle, supplements, date of origin, frequency, price, size, publisher, place of publication, and indexes, if any. Perhaps the most useful guide to magazines, especially of the Americas and the British Empire.

"An outstanding feature, added in 1956 by Graves, is the notation of the many indexing and abstracting services: it indicates in which general periodical index each is indexed or abstracted . . . every user . . . will be grateful to the compiler for bringing together in convenient compass so many titles, especially those less easily accessible to the searcher, such as Slavic Publications. By the aid of the UNION LIST OF SERIALS the student may now easily locate, in some American libraries, sets of periodicals brought to his notice by this directory"—(LIBRARY QUARTERLY, 1932, 432–435).

To Periodicals and Learned Journals

Annual Library Index, 1905–1910. Including Periodicals, American and English; Essays, Book-Chapters, Bibliographies, Necrology, and an Index to Dates of Principal Events. New York: Publishers' Weekly, 1906–1911. 6 vols. o.p.

Differs from its predecessor, the ANNUAL LITERARY INDEX, mainly in this, that its index to periodicals contained authors, titles, and subjects in one alphabet, instead of two distinct subject and author lists. For author entries, superseded in 1911 by the AMERICAN LIBRARY ANNUAL; for subject entries, it is now virtually superseded by READERS' GUIDE and the INTERNATIONAL INDEX. Still useful for some author entries for 1905–1906.

"The field of periodical literature has been very efficiently cared for, these many years by first the CUMULATIVE INDEX which, later combined with the READERS' GUIDE, is now furnishing all the help that any library could ask along the lines of periodical literature"—(PUBLIC LIBRARY, VOL. 10, March, 1905, 127).

Annual Literary Index, 1892–1904: Including Periodicals, American and English; Essays, Book-Chapters, etc. New York: Publishers' Weekly, 1893–1905. 13 vols.

Each volume contains: (1) subject index to periodicals; (2) subject index to general literature; (3) author index to periodical and other literature; (4) bibliographies; (5) necrology; (6) index to dates of main events.

The composite annual index comprehends among the six divisions of the work four distinct indexes: a subject index, an annual continuation of POOLE'S INDEX, which indexes the same periodicals in the same way and forms the basis for the five-year supplements; (2) a subject index to essays, a continuation of the A.L.A. Index; (3) a needed author index, lacking in POOLE'S INDEX; and (4) an index to dates, serving practically as an index to newspapers.

"Undoubtedly this index will be found a necessity in even the smaller libraries. . . . Nothing could do more to enable a librarian to make the most of a small library"—(LIBRARY JOURNAL, VOL. 17, 1892, 7).

Annual Magazine Subject Index. Boston: F. W. Faxon Co., Inc., 1908–1949. 41 vols.

The first volume, entitled MAGAZINE SUBJECT INDEX, indexed 79 periodicals (44 from their first issue to Dec. 31, 1907; 35, for the year 1907). The subsequent volumes, entitled ANNUAL MAGAZINE SUBJECT INDEX, are annual supplements.

Provides abbreviated title of periodical, volume, date, inclusive paging, and indication of illustrations, portraits, maps, and plans.

". . . opens a new field of research because it indexes nothing included in POOLE'S INDEX, THE LIBRARY INDEX, or the READER'S GUIDE. Originally intended to be simply a cumulation in one alphabet of the four quarterly installments in the BULLETIN OF BIBLIOGRAPHY for 1907, it has been broadened to include the back years of many periodicals and those which heretofore were not included in the BULLETIN"— (LIBRARY JOURNAL, XXXIII, July, 1908, 164).

Book Review Digest, 1905–. New York: The H. W. Wilson Company, 1905—.

An index of selected book reviews in seventy or more English and American periodicals (principally the latter), providing in many cases brief excerpts from the reviews, indicating the length of the review in number of words, and the negative or positive tone of the review. For each book entered, it gives the author, title, paging, publisher, price, a brief descriptive note, and exact references to the periodicals in which the notices or reviews appeared.

Primarily useful for the general layman and the undergraduate, because of the character of the book listed and the character of the periodical from which the review is derived—learned journals being only occasionally the sources.

"The summaries are well done, though a tendency toward the favorable point of view is perhaps to be observed"—(LIBRARY JOURNAL, XXX, April, 1905, 245).

Catholic Periodical Index: A Cumulative Author and Subject Index to a Selected List of Catholic Periodicals. New York: Catholic Library Association, 1939–.

The 1930–1933 publication forms the first permanent volume and supersedes the earlier two volumes for 1930–1931. The 1939–1943 volume, published in 1945, represents the second cumulation. The 1943–1948 cumulation appeared in 1955. The 1934–1938 cumulation remains unpublished.

"This service . . . is one for which we cannot be too grateful. A pioneer in its field, it is indeed an event in American Catholic literature. If librarians have realized its need, research and editorial workers have been no less hampered for lack of it, and it is already proving itself of inestimable value to them. Modeled mainly on that excellent prototype, H. W. Wilson's READERS' GUIDE TO PERIODICAL LITERATURE, it is a difficult task well done"—(CATHOLIC WORLD, VOL. 131, June, 1930, 378).

"The uses of the index are many and varied. Aside from constant use and research workers' attention, it is copiously useful in enabling educators to keep abreast of all current literature on subjects on which they are interested"—(ECCLESIASTICAL REVIEW, VOL. 82, April, 1930, 445).

International Index to Periodicals: A quarterly Guide to Periodical Literature in the Social Sciences and Humanities. New York: Wilson, 1955–. Vol. 43–.

The subtitle of this index, when first published in 1907, was: "Devoted Chiefly to the Humanities and Science." The first volume indexed only seventy-four periodicals, but the subsequent volumes were enlarged by the inclusion of forty-five serials, mainly foreign, previously indexed by the analytic cards issued by the American Library Association Publishing Board. Beginning with volume forty-three, scientific, psychological, and foreign language periodicals were dropped, and fifty-three new periodicals, in the fields of the humanities and social sciences in the English language were added. Among the subjects now emphasized are language, literature, anthropology, archaeology, geography, and history; and economics, sociology, political science, labor, public opinion, philosophy, religion, musicology, and the theater arts. The title varies: volumes one and two, READERS' GUIDE TO PERIODICAL LITERATURE SUPPLEMENTS; volume three, INTERNATIONAL INDEX TO PERIODICALS.

"Of these, the one of most interest, perhaps, in the large library, is the new permanent volume of the INTERNATIONAL INDEX which appears with the imprint date of 1924, though not ready until 1925. It is much larger than the preceding cumulation of 1916–1919, containing 600 more pages than the earlier issue and indexing some 275 periodicals as against 126 in 1916–1919. Of these 275 periodicals, 185 are in English, 33 in French, 49 in German, while a few titles in Dutch, Spanish, Italian, and Swedish complete the list. . . . The indispensable index for the university library"—(LIBRARY JOURNAL, January 1, 1925, 13).

Nineteenth Century Readers' Guide to Periodical Literature, 1890–1899. Supplementary indexing, 1900–1901. Helen Grant Cushing and Adah V. Morris, eds. New York: The H. W. Wilson Company, 1944. 2 vols.

An author, subject, and illustrator index to the contents of fifty-one periodicals principally—for thirty-seven, actually—for the years 1890–1899. The other periodicals are carried forward as far as 1922.

The periodicals indexed are mainly general and literary. Short stories, novels, and plays are indexed under author and title; reviews of books are listed under author entry only; more than 13,000 poems are listed by title, with a full entry under the author's name. A retrospective supplement to READERS' GUIDE.

Pool's Index to Periodical Literature, 1802–1821. Rev. ed. Boston: Houghton Mifflin Company, 1891. 2 vols. Supplements, 1887–1908, 5 vols.

The pioneer index to American and English periodicals and, though now discontinued, still significantly useful, covering as it does the longest period (105 years) and constituting the largest index of its kind—including the greatest number of items (590,-000 articles; 12,241 volumes; 470 English and American periodicals).

Users of the index should remember that: (1) it has no author entries; (2) articles which have a distinct subject are entered under that subject; (3) articles which have no subject are entered under the first word of the title (excepting articles); (4) book reviews are entered either under subject, if the book has a definite subject, or under the author's name, if it does not have a distinct subject. Specific references are made to maps, portraits, and other illustrations, as well as to bibliographies.

"It is hardly necessary to urge upon the attention of . . . colleges and academies the utility of making POOLE'S INDEX available for their senior students"—(CATHOLIC WORLD, January, 1890, 558).

"As is truly said in nearly every article, there is no need to enlarge upon its importance; it is something eagerly desired by every librarian, and something we have been looking for every year, only to be constantly disappointed"—(THE AMERICAN LIBRARY JOURNAL, April 30, 1877, 279–287).

Readers' Guide to Periodical Literature, 1900—. New York: The H. W. Wilson Company, 1905—.

The major guide to general periodicals. Initially, it indexed a small group of popular periodicals. But by 1903 it had absorbed the CUMULATIVE INDEX; and by 1911 it had taken over the function of the ANNUAL LIBRARY INDEX. Today it indexes as many as 125 periodicals, mostly general and popular, although a few scientific and scholarly publications are included.

Among its basic features are: (1) full dictionary cataloguing of all articles (author, subject, and, when necessary, title; (2) uniformity of entries; (3) catalog subject headings, instead of catchword subject; (4) full reference information (volume and page, and to exact date and inclusive paging); (5) cumulative features designed to keep the index up to date; (6) indexing of book reviews through 1904, after which they are to be found in the BOOK REVIEW DIGEST.

"Poetry, which is ignored by POOLE'S except as a subject treated of, is carefully recorded by the new index. And another point: each entry of poetry or other articles gives not only the volume and page of the magazine, but also the date"—(NEW YORK TIMES, February 3, 1906, 72).

Review of Reviews: Index to the Periodicals of 1890–1902. London and New York: Review of Reviews, 1891–1903. 13 vols. o.p.

The title of the first volume is, ANNUAL INDEX OF PERIODICALS AND PHOTOGRAPHS FOR 1890. The title of the second, third, and fourth volumes is, INDEX TO THE PERIODICAL LITERATURE OF THE WORLD.

While it contains some author entries, it is essentially a broad subject index, providing for each entry a brief title, periodical, volume, month, and page reference, and an exact reference to the REVIEW OF REVIEWS where a summary or other notice of the article is to be found. Since it covers a number of periodicals, especially British ones, that are not indexed in Poole's, it serves as a supplement to the latter work.

"The present volume is estimated to contain about 12,000 articles, and is as useful, practical, and detailed as could be expected"—(LIBRARY JOURNAL, XXIX, 1904, 102).

"The overall arrangement is good and its inclusions comprehensive. The work is a 'must' for any American library, although its speciality seems to be that of British periodicals"—(LIBRARY JOURNAL, XXVII, 1902, 1029).

Saturday Review of Literature.

The REVIEW is the most embracive American weekly devoted primarily to the review of books. General and semi-popular works are reviewed by professional reviewers; the scholarly books are reviewed by specialists. In addition, the SATURDAY REVIEW contains feature articles on many subjects; (in the first issue), a section devoted to science reports, research developments, social aspects, etc.; (in the final issue) a lengthy recording section with popular and classical record reviews, as well as articles on artists, music, and composers.

"Its success, however, should not be experimental in view of the extraordinary increase of popular interest in the field of literary discussion and combat"—(NEW YORK TIMES, August 1, 1934, 5).

Subject Index to Periodicals. 1915—. London: Library Association, 1919—.

An English index which was first issued as the ATHENAEUM SUBJECT INDEX, the outcome of a resolution passed at a meeting of the Library Association in 1913, advocating the resumption of an index to periodicals on the lines of POOLE'S. Until 1922, the indexes were divided into classified lists according to broad subjects (e.g., theology and philosophy; historical, political, and economic sciences; education and child welfare). Since 1926, when the publication was revived, there has been a single alphabetical indexing, principally by subjects.

"The index is not altogether inclusive, but perhaps it was not intended to be so. There are many insertions referring to subjects in American periodicals, which perhaps could not be otherwise, for the language of America is of the Modern European" —(PUBLIC LIBRARIES, VOL. XXVI, 1921).

To Books

American Catalogue of Books, 1876–1910. New York: Publisher's Weekly, 1876–1910. Reprinted in 1941 by Peter Smith.

The 1938 publication of the AMERICAN CATALOGUE reprints and continues the BIBLIOTHECA AMERICANA of Roorbach, and brings the work down to 1861; the 1941 publication was compiled by Lynds E. Jones and published in reprint form by Peter Smith in 1941.

The standard American list for the period covered. Aims to include all books published in the United States which were in print and for sale to the general public on July 1, 1876, excepting: local directories, periodicals, sheet music, unbound maps, tracts, and miscellaneous cheap pamphlets.

"Reference librarians are particularly grateful for the reprint of POOLE'S INDEX now available complete except for the annual library service of 1907–1910, but an even greater debt of gratitude is due the publishers for helping to make available the complete chain of American national bibliography. Already Kelly's AMERICAN CATALOG, previously unobtainable for love or money, is available in two volumes at a price of $7.50 a volume. Roorbach's BIBLIOTHECA AMERICANA, four volumes, is listed at a total cost of $20.00, and now comes a most welcome P.S. from Peter Smith: 'We expect to announce shortly our project for a reprint of the AMERICAN CATALOG OF BOOKS, 1876–1910—the whole blessed business'"—(WILSON LIBRARY BULLETIN, XIII, 482).

"The AMERICAN CATALOGUE, that monumental undertaking begun by Frederick Leypoldt in the 1870's . . . is being reissued in photographic reprint by Peter Smith. . . . The availability of this 13-volume series will be a boon to any number of librarians and their users, and to the rare book trade. The volumes have long been out of print, and though very substantially printed with wide margins for rebinding they have been difficult to pick up for many years"—(PUBLISHER'S WEEKLY, May 24, 1941, 2070).

"If we do not praise the linotype for its mechanical beauty in this instance, its aid to bibliography ensures full devotion"—(THE NATION, January–June, 1905, 501).

American Library Association Catalog: An Annotated Basic List of 10,000 Books. Chicago: American Library Association, 1926–. 1295 p. o.p.

First published in 1893, followed by a second edition in 1904, and then by supplements covering the period 1904–1911 and 1912–1921. A classified list, arranged in the main according to the Dewey Decimal System, and providing, for United States publications since 1893, author, title, date, paging, publisher's name, Library of Congress card number, and an annotation to indicate scope and value. Its two main limitations are perhaps: (1) omission of materials published outside of the United States; (2) annotations, though often quotations from other comment, are given without an exact indication of source. Contains separate lists for biography and fiction and for children's books.

"For the reference worker the full author, title, and subject index is an excellent tool. It is a valuable for all libraries, book stores, schools, and to anyone wanting an authoritative survey"—(BOOKLIST, 23:60, November, 1926).

"Is well indexed with reference to author, title, subject. Well printed and bound. Will be the standard of selection for many years to come"—(WISCONSIN LIBRARY BULLETIN, 22:239, December, 1926).

"The biography section is a treasure house of good reading. It is impossible to criticize it. . . . A curious omission is a statement of policy with regard to the inclusion of out-of-print books. . . ."—(LIBRARY JOURNAL, December 1, 1926).

"The A.L.A. CATALOGUE is in a class by itself as an aid to book selections for the American library. For this purpose it is indispensable and invaluable. Its use as a reference tool would have been increased, however, by the giving of authorities for the quoted or adapted annotations, and by a more frequent indication of dates of first publication where recent reprints are chosen for inclusion"—(LIBRARY JOURNAL, VOL. LII, 82).

American Library Association Index to General Literature. 2d ed. Chicago: American Library Association Publications Board, 1901. 679 p. Supplement, 1914, 223 p.

The basic volume deals with books in English published before 1900; the supplement deals with works published between 1900 and 1910. The predecessor to the current ESSAY AND GENERAL LITERATURE INDEX, it aims to do for books of essays and general literature what POOLE'S INDEX does for periodicals. The works indexed belong to the following groups: (1) historical, literary, and biographical essays; (2) books of travel; (3) reports and publications of literary, historical, and sociological societies; miscellaneous works. Its two most serious shortcomings: includes only works in English; indexes by catchword subject, rather than, as its successor does, by a combination of entries.

Annals of English Literature, 1475–1925: The Principal Publications of Each Year with an Alphabetical Index of Authors and Their Works. Oxford: Clarendon Press, 1935. 345 p.

"Sound in scholarship and admirable in organization of its vast contents, this reference volume increasingly stirs the reader as he turns the pages with thoughts of the endless patience, care and hard work that went into the making. . . . As a reference work for any one interested in literature and a handbook for literary students, the volume will be invaluable"—(COMMONWEAL, March 20, 1936).

"No more useful work on English literature than this has been produced for a considerable time"—(SPECULUM, 156:320, Feb. 21, 1936).

"It can be read straightforward, with both profit and pleasure, a conspectus of the expansion of English literature . . .

and it can be worked backwards from the index in the process of checking dates of author and of books"—(TIMES, London, Feb., 1936, 97).

Essay and General Literature Index, 1900–1933: An Index to about 40,000 Essays and Articles in 2,144 Volumes of Collections of Essays and Miscellaneous Works. New York: The H. W. Wilson Company, 1934. 1952 p.

1934–1940: An Index to 23,090 Essays and Articles in 1,241 Volumes of Collections of Essays and Miscellaneous Works. New York: The H. W. Wilson Company, 1941. 1362 p.

1941–1947; An Index to 32,226 Essays and Articles in 2,023 Volumes of Collections of Essays and Miscellaneous Works. New York: The H. W. Wilson Company, 1948. 1908 p.

The 1948–1954 cumulation was published in 1955.

An author, subject, and, occasionally, title index to collections of essays in all fields, as well as an index to some miscellaneous works which have reference value, such as collective biography. Provides: (1) list of essays by given author; (2) authorship of an essay when only the title is known; (3) analytical material on a given subject, particularly in areas in which there exist no solid treatments; (4) biographical and critical material; (5) criticisms of individual books; (6) different works in which an essay may be found.

A reviewer of the basic volume notes that: "While only books published since 1900 are included, the material to be found in collections by various authors includes not only the work of modern essayists but also a great many essays by the earlier standard essayists, such as Addison, Bacon, Carlyle, Emerson, Hazlitt, and Lamb"—(BOOK REVIEW DIGEST, 1935, 295).

Guide to Catholic Literature, 1888–1940. Detroit: Romig, 1940. 1240 p.

Volume two covers the years 1940–1944; volume three, the years, 1944–1948; volume four, the years 1948–1951. The work now appears annually with four-year cumulations.

An author-subject-title index in one alphabet of books and booklets, in all languages and in all subjects by Catholics and of particular interest to Catholics.

"The format does not make for legibility or for quick reference use. The main entries are in bold type, but the items appearing under each entry are not adequately spaced. . . . While some cross references are used, they are neither consistent nor adequate. While some foreign language publications are included, the list is by no means complete. . . . In spite of the numerous inaccuracies and its incompleteness, as an index to works on general subjects it is recommended for Catholics and for large public libraries"—(SUBSCRIPTION BOOKS BULLETIN, April, 1941).

SERIALS

Ephemeral Materials

Pamphlets, booklets, brochures, circulars, bulletins, charts, posters, and similar materials at times constitute a significant supplement to book, periodical, and newspaper content. The basic index to such information is the VERTICAL FILE SERVICE CATALOG; an annotated subject list (issued monthly except August) of inexpensively published materials, which gives title, author, page, reference, publisher, and price.

Newspapers

The New York Times, 1851–. New York: New Times Company.

The most comprehensive newspaper in America. Originally a four-page, handset sheet, its Sunday issue now exceeds three hundred pages. It is supplemented by the SUNDAY TIMES BOOK REVIEW and the TIMES MAGAZINE. Among its special features are: reproductions of full texts of treatises and pronouncements, speeches, and other significant documents; and departments devoted to book reviews, education, art, music, theater, and industrial activities.

". . . learned, but not pedantic; objective, but never indifferent; detailed and painstaking, but not intolerant; forthright in politics, but rarely partisan; world-wide in vision, coverage, and influence, but always American"—(MEYER BERGER, THE STORY OF THE NEW YORK TIMES, 565).

Its hundred years of success are "proof of the soundness of the theory of responsible journalism"—(THE CHRISTIAN CENTURY, October 3, 1951, 115–116).

The TIMES continues to be an example of devotion to the reporting of news almost as a "public service to the world community"—(THE SATURDAY REVIEW OF LITERATURE, October 6, 1951, 26).

London Times, 1788—. London: The Times.

The LONDON TIMES was founded in 1788 by the Walter family. In 1906 there was added a literary supplement, similar in appearance to a representative American Sunday supplement. The TIMES is generally considered to be the foremost newspaper published in the English language.

"It has written the history of the British Empire and of the modern world with a breadth of view and a sense of perspective which its keenest critics must concede and admire. The TIMES foreign correspondents have always been men with ability and much training. . . . it has so long risen above the level of partisanship and has so clearly and successfully interpreted British opinion, that it has come to be regarded as a national institution"—(THE OUTLOOK, Vol. 88, 66).

In recent years the paper's influence has visibly declined. "Still, it retains a prestige greater than any other newspaper. . . . its supreme reputation was won by its unexampled corps of foreign correspondents. . . . Above and beyond all these titles to distinction, there was for years a quality in the TIMES which really gained for it the name of 'The Thunderer.' This was its ability to hit English public opinion between wind and water. When it spoke, its voice was really the voice of England" —(NATION, VOL. 86, 18–25).

Learned Journals

American Literature, 1929—. North Carolina: Duke University Press, 1929—.

AMERICAN LITERATURE, the only research organ exclusively devoted to the study of the literature of the United States, first appeared in March, 1929. It is published by the Duke University Press; editorially sponsored by the American Literature Group of the MLA; and is indexed in the BIOGRAPHY INDEX and the INTERNATIONAL INDEX. It publishes only original papers of a critical, historical, or bibliographical nature, as well as a checklist of articles in the area of its special interest and a list of dissertations in progress or completed.

"There could be no better evidence of the new life that has recently come into the scholarly study of the literature of our own country than the establishment of AMERICAN LITERATURE, A Journal of Literary History, Criticism, and Bibliography. If we may judge by the 111 pages of this first number (33 of which are given to reviews by distinguished scholars), the new quarterly will not only stimulate investigation and offer it a needed outlet, but will also maintain standards of accuracy, thoroughness, and good writing, together with breadth of outlook, in a field where these qualities have sometimes been to seek"—(MODERN LANGUAGE NOTES, VOL. 44, 420).

American Journal of Philology, 1880—.

The first ten volumes of the AJP—completed in 1880—provided early evidence of sound learning and a mass of valuable linguistic facts. An important tool to scholars. Publishes reviews. Its special field is Roman and Greek studies.

English Literary History: A Journal of English Literary History. Baltimore: The Tudor and Stuart Club, The Johns Hopkins University, 1934—.

Not detailed in its treatment of literary backgrounds, but provides a well-balanced, unbiased, and scholarly handling of literary personnages. Publishes no reviews. From 1934 to 1950, it provided in its March issue a critical bibliography of the Romantic movement. In 1950, "The Romantic Movement: A Selective and Critical Bibliography," began to appear in the April issue of PHILOLOGICAL QUARTERLY.

"This attractively printed periodical is unique in several respects: it is edited by young men, it is sponsored by a university literary club, it contains no reviews, it appears three times a year, it costs only $1.50. The length of time that a learned article dealing with English literature must wait before publication makes clear the need of another magazine in this field. The first two issues of ELH promise a journal of high standards which should be supported by all those interested in the scholarly study of English literature"—(MODERN LANGUAGE NOTES, VOL. 49, 551).

English Studies. A Publication of the English Association. London: John Murray, 1948–.

A journal of English letters and philology (not to be confused with ENGLISCHE STUDIEN, which has been published at Leipzig since 1877 and is sometimes abbreviated EST or ENG STUD). Publishes no reviews. ENGLISH STUDIES replaces ESSAYS AND STUDIES, which was published annually from 1910 to 1948.

"Two articles which have little or nothing to do with English studies fill rather more than a quarter of this volume. In 'The Character and Private Life of Edmund Burke' Sir Philip Magnus writes interestingly and at length of the politician and his finances, mentioning the author and his works only briefly and by the way. The other five contributions are genuine English studies, although of varying merit. But taken as a whole the volume does not illustrate any clear conception of the characteristic preoccupations and necessary limits of English studies. It is regrettable that its apparently aimless eclecticism should have the official approval of the English Association"—(NEW SERIES, 2, 1951, 294–296).

Essays in Criticism. Oxford: Blackwell Press, 1951–.

The basic sections of this quarterly—it appears in January, April, July, and October—are: "Feature Articles," "Book Reviews," and "The Critical Forum." A representative issue (April, 1960) ranged from Shakespeare and Coleridge to James Joyce. "The Critical Forum" is a kind of free court in which scholars and would-be scholars exchange volleys of opinion.

"ESSAYS IN CRITICISM resembles SCRUTINY more than any other English periodical, but it is a less unified magazine, with a less distinctive tone of voice. . . . The flavor of the magazine as a whole is that of a 'new' academicism rather too spryly conscious of not being the 'old' academicism"—(TIMES LITERARY SUPPLEMENT, 1953, 353).

"If the admirably high standard and variety of critical writing manifest in this first number should be maintained, the new journal will deserve a much longer life than the probationary three years. An editorial board representative of English studies both at Oxford and other universities seems to give assurance that it will be maintained"—(THE TIMES LITERARY SUPPLEMENT, Feb. 16, 1951, 105).

Folklore, 1890—. London: William Glaisher, Ltd., 1890—.

FOLKLORE is the result of the merging in 1890 of the ARCHAEOLOGICAL REVIEW and the FOLKLORE JOURNAL. It publishes reviews and notes of interesting events in the field of folklore, as well as news of meetings. It is indexed in the MAGAZINE SUBJECT INDEX. Its articles lack the scholarly tone of its American counterpart.

"It appears to us, so far as the present issue may be considered a fair sample, that the Folklore Society has got the best of the bargain, and there is not much room left for archaeology proper. We are no doubt promised the revival of some of the special features of the ARCHAEOLOGICAL REVIEW, and we hope that the promise will be kept"—(NOTES AND QUERIES, VOL. 9, April 19, 1890, 320).

Huntington Library Bulletin. Cambridge, Massachusetts, 1931–1937. 11 vols.

The Huntington Library was required by trust indentures to render its possessions accessible to scholars and students engaged in research or creative work, and to this end the HUNTINGTON BULLETIN was published. Specifically, the BULLETIN aimed: to particularize the resources of the Library; to give bibliographies and other information about its collections, especially texts of rare unpublished manuscripts; list the research articles which resulted from the studies made from bibliographic material; include short notes of interest to the library and its staff. The BULLETIN was at first intended to be an occasional number, rather than a periodical publication.

"In communion with bibliographers and students of English and American culture everywhere, we are glad to welcome the HUNTINGTON LIBRARY BULLETIN. . . . If we may judge from the contents of the first number, the execution of this program will be followed with the keenest interest by scholars"—(MODERN PHILOLOGY, Vol. 29, 375).

"The publication of the HUNTINGTON LIBRARY BULLETIN is therefore a notable event in American librarianship. More than 100 pages, approximately one-half of the first number, are given over to matter which should form a part of the working data of every advanced reference worker"—(LIBRARY QUARTERLY, 1932, 87).

The HUNTINGTON LIBRARY BULLETIN was succeeded by the HUNTINGTON LIBRARY QUARTERLY, published at San Marino, California, 1937—.

Journal of American Folklore, 1888—. Philadelphia: The University of Pennsylvania, 1888—.

The JOURNAL OF AMERICAN FOLKLORE was founded mainly to collect and preserve the fast—vanishing memoirs of American folklore (of the English, the Negroes in the South, and the Indian tribes in the north as well as that of Mexico and French Canada), and to publish the special studies of them.

"The Society is to be congratulated upon the substantial and diversfied contents and attractive appearance of the two numbers which have already appeared. It is understood that the American Society's membership has already outstripped that of its much older English sister"—(MODERN LANGUAGE NOTES, VOL. 3, 1888, 471).

Journal of English and Germanic Philology. Urbana, Illinois: The University of Illinois Press, 1897—.

As the JOURNAL OF GERMANIC PHILOLOGY, Volumes I to IV were published at Bloomington, Indiana, and Volume V at Evanston, Illinois, between the years 1903 to 1905. Since 1906 it has been published by the University of Illinois, at Urbana, Illinois, as the JOURNAL OF ENGLISH AND GERMANIC PHILOLOGY. Contains articles on English, German, and Scandinavian languages and literatures, books reviewed and received (April issue), and comments of the reviewers.

Although it is issued as a quarterly, there are occasional supplements containing more extensive contributions which the journal deems worthy of publication. The contributions are received from international scholars, and the subject matter often varies and extends to all of the languages and the fields of the humanities.

"This new periodical begins its career on a well-founded plan . . . none but trained and competent experts will be solicited as contributors, but the journal will be made beneficial for the progressive teacher of any level and for all students of Germanics. . . . The JOURNAL will have a purely pedagogical purpose, and will establish a relation between pure and applied philology. . . . It will also give American investigators a hearing before the whole Germanic world"—(THE CRITIC, VOL. 30, January–June, 1897).

Modern Language Notes. Baltimore: The Johns Hopkins University Press, 1886—.

Published monthly from November to June. An index to Volumes I–L, edited by H. H. Shapiro, was published in 1935. Publishes reviews.

Modern Language Quarterly. Seattle, Washington: University of Washington Press, 1940—.

A scholarly journal devoted to the perpetuation of philology and the modern languages through the encouragement of research in all the areas of the humanities. As an illustration of its scope, one might note that a typical issue contains a cultural interpretation of Beowulf, an offering of the Folger Shakespeare Library, and a study of Herman Melville's stories. Publishes book reviews and indexes books received. Articles are not signed. An Arthurian Bibliography beginning with the years 1936–1939 was inaugurated with the first edition and continues to the present.

"A new journal to which STUDIES IN PHILOLOGY extends a welcome is MODERN LANGUAGE QUARTERLY, published by the University of Washington Press and edited by Ray Heffner. The unusual range and policy of this journal is doubtless suggested by the contents of its first issue. . . . Its one hundred twenty-six pages contain ten articles and four reviews"—(STUDIES IN PHILOLOGY, VOLUME 37, 563–564).

Modern Language Review. Cambridge, England: 1905—. Supersedes MODERN LANGUAGE QUARTERLY, London, 1897–1904. 7 vols.

Devoted to the study of medieval and of modern literature and philology. Volumes I to X are indexed in Volume X; Volumes XI to XX are indexed in Volume XX; and Volumes XXI to XXX are indexed in Volume XXX. "It is part of the justification of the REVIEW that it has sought to be an organ of international scholarship and thought. . . (and the growth of it) in its fifty years service has accompanied and closely reflected the growth of organized modern language study in British universities." Publishes reviews.

Modern Philology: A Journal Devoted to Research in Modern Languages and Literatures. Chicago: The University of Chicago Press, 1903—.

A quarterly journal interested in all significant developments in the fields of literary study. It ordinarily does not treat of linguistics, but articles of general interest in this field are sometimes accepted. Since May, 1933, it has published an annual Victorian bibliography, listing American and foreign publication in the period, and frequently citing and quoting from reviews of more significant works.

Since each volume begins in one year and carries over into the next, it is necessary to give a double-year date. In citing a particular article, however, it is quite proper to give only the year in which the particular article appeared.

Notes and Queries. London, 1849—.

A weekly publication devoted to the presentation of notes—little articles submitted by readers and scholars—and queries—questions sent in by readers.

From November, 1849 to December, 1923, there were twelve series, comprising twelve half-year volumes each, with an index for every series. Beginning in January, 1924, the series number was dropped. An index to Volumes CXLV to CLVI (July, 1923 to June, 1929) was followed by one to Volumes CLXII to CLXVIII. Publishes reviews.

Philological Quarterly: A Journal Devoted to Scholarly Investigation in the Classical and Modern Languages and Literatures. Iowa City: State University of Iowa Press, 1922—.

Embraces Greek and Latin as well as the modern European languages, but it does not publish articles which are primarily concerned with non-European languages or their literatures. In general, it leans toward articles on specific problems or interpretations in language or literature.

The July issue features a bibliography of current English literature for the period 1660–1800, and since 1950 the April issue contains a bibliography of the Romantic Movement, a feature taken over from the March issue of ENGLISH LITERARY HISTORY. In recent issues, book reviews appear to have been eliminated.

"Under the competent editorial management of Professor Hardin Craig, its scholarly character is abundantly assured; and the cooperation of the chosen associate editors . . . strongly ratify that assurance. The uniting of classical and modern language studies has a fresh significance at this time. This will enable the new periodical to assume the attractive and no less important function of expounding and contributing to the illumination of one of the principal chapters in present-day educational and cultural problems"—(MODERN LANGUAGE NOTES, VOLUME 37, 254).

Publications of the Modern Language Association of America. Baltimore, 1884—.

The first issue in 1884 comprised fifty pages. Current issues frequently exceed three hundred pages. The first three volumes contained articles on pedagogy, but the emphasis since then has been in the areas of modern languages and literature. Since 1921, the March issue has carried a bibliography; this is now carried in the Supplement. Until 1956 the bibliography was limited to American writers of books and articles in the field of modern languages; in 1957 the bibliography was broadened to include English, Dutch, French, German, Spanish, Italian, Portuguese, and Scandinavian. It does not publish reviews.

"Volume I, TRANSACTIONS OF THE MODERN LANGUAGE ASSOCIATION OF AMERICA, covered the years 1884–1885. Volumes II–III, called TRANSACTIONS AND PROCEEDINGS, covered the years 1886–1887. Volume IV, called PUBLICATIONS OF THE MODERN LANGUAGE ASSOCIATION OF AMERICA, was divided into four numbers for 1888–1889. Thereafter the serial was a regular quarterly under the title PUBLICATIONS OF THE MODERN LANGUAGE ASSOCIATION OF AMERICA, with a cover title PMLA in recent years. There has been a distinguished editorship: A. Marshall Elliott, founder of MLA and its first secretary, James W. Bright, Charles H. Grandgent, William Guild Howard, Charton Brown, and Percy Waldron Long"—(MOTT, A HISTORY OF AMERICAN MAGAZINES, 1865–1885, Volume 3, 236).

Review of English Studies: A Quarterly Journal of English Literature and Language. Oxford: Clarendon Press, 1925—.

A typical issue contains: notes and short notices, book reviews, a summary of periodical literature, and a list of publications received.

Speculum: A Quarterly Journal of Mediaeval Studies. Cambridge, Massachusetts: The Mediaeval Academy of America, 1926—.

Each issue contains a bibliography of the periodical literature in the mediaeval period that appeared during the preceding quarter; and it often publishes articles intended to illuminate neglected areas and to open up new fields of research. It is indexed by the ART INDEX and the INTERNATIONAL INDEX; publishes reviews.

In addition to articles such as "The Ancient Classics in the Medieval Libraries," a typical number might contain: book reviews; a bibliography of periodical literature organized by subjects, such as fine arts, Dante, language, folklore, philosophy, religion, books received, sometimes with a few words of description; publications of the Medieval Academy.

"Its intention is to stimulate further researches and more extensive publication in the medieval field, to serve as a coordinating bureau for all activities in America concerning life and thought of the Middle Ages, and to foster international cooperation in the same field. . . . This initial number of SPECULUM is of high quality and admirable appearance"—(AMERICAN HISTORICAL REVIEW, VOLUME 31, NUMBER 3, 609).

"The officers of the Academy and the editors of the journal are men who have won distinction in the classics, in history, in architecture, and in modern languages. This is a heartening fact, since one great need of modern scholarship is collaboration among workers whose fields have much in common, but who are kept apart by the artificial 'departments' of college catalogues. There is also reason for congratulation in the fact that both medieval specialists and scholars whose primary interests lie outside the Middle Ages may find, in SPECULUM, monographs, notes, and reviews which deal with a single great period of human culture"—(MODERN LANGUAGE NOTES, VOLUME 41, 271).

Studies in Philology. Chapel Hill, North Carolina: University of North Carolina Press, 1906—.

A journal of special interest to students of the Renaissance period. Does not publish reviews, but does publish in each April issue a Renaissance bibliography. There is an index for Volumes I to XXV.

"STUDIES IN PHILOLOGY attracted the attention of scholars all over the country from its beginning . . . gained new importance and became recognized as one of the leading scholarly journals, internationally as well as nationally"—(STUDIES IN PHILOLOGY, VOLUME 42, 1945).

Times Literary Supplement. London, 1902—.

A weekly publication, with an annual index. The "Correspondence" columns contain many items of interest to scholars. It publishes reviews.

BIBLIOGRAPHY

Guides and Manuals of Theory and History

Bibliographical Services Throughout The World. Paris: UNESCO, 1955–. Vol. I. Annual.

Embraces two separate reports on the development and bibliographical services throughout the world. Principal arrangement is by continent; subordinate arrangement is by country. Describes "the national bibliography, official publication lists, union catalogs, bibliographical publications, bibliographical committees and institutes.

BINNS, NORMAN E.
An Introduction to Historical Bibliography. London: Association of Assistant Librarians, 1953. 370 p.

A history of bookmaking, including chapters on publishing and bookselling, copyright, and development of book trade bibliography. Bibliographies are appended to each chapter; contains an index.

BOWERS, FREDSON.
Principles of Bibliographical Description. Princeton: Princeton University Press, 1949. 505 p.

Aims to expound a system of bibliography based upon what is considered to be the most acceptable current practice. Not a survey of methods and procedures, but a comprehensive treatment of analytical bibliography as applied to the description of books. Includes the principles of describing incunabula, as well as those which relate to the description of English and American books of the sixteenth through the twentieth centuries. Complements McKerrow's INTRODUCTION TO BIBLIOGRAPHY. The Appendices contain samples of bibliographical description, a digest of formulary, and the applications of the formulary notation to incunabula.

"Professor Bowers has written a formidable work . . . one that deserves careful study by those producing detailed bibliographies. . . . Notwithstanding some faults, the book will be of great value to bibliographers if it is borne in mind that their first aim is to describe editions, issues, etc., as well as they can, rather than to elaborate a system of symbols not easily understood"—(LONDON TIMES LITERARY SUPPLEMENT, Sept. 29, 1950).

"It is regretable that the index is not more comprehensive . . . a completed list of abbreviations and symbols . . . would have been desirable"—(LIBRARY JOURNAL, VOLUME 75, 1040).

BUHLER, CURT F.
Standards of Bibliographical Description. Philadelphia: University of Pennsylvania Press, 1949. 120 p.

A series of lectures presented under the Rosenthal Fellowship by three distinguished bibliographers, each of whom sets forth a distinct approach to a common problem: Curt Buhler, "Incunabula"; James McManaway, "Early English Literature"; Lawrence C. Wroth, "Early American Literature." The lectures constitute the 1946–1947 presentations under the A.S.W. Rosenbach Fellowship in Bibliography.

"Careful proofreading adds to the attractiveness of this well designed volume. And since it is a volume of theory not primarily of reference, the lack of an index is perhaps endurable. . . . The first and longest lecture, by Dr. Buhler, is possibly the most stimulating and satisfying"—(LIBRARY QUARTERLY, VOLUME 21, 1951, 65–66).

"Some of the most distinguished bibliographical essays published in North America in recent years were originally delivered as Rosenbach Lectures in Bibliography at the University of Pennsylvania. The three studies in the current volume . . . are no exception to this statement. . . . The wealth of ideas in STANDARDS OF BIBLIOGRAPHICAL DESCRIPTION will form the basis for important studies in the immediate future"—(INTERNATIONAL LIBRARY REVIEW, 1952–1953, 176–177).

ESDAILE, ARUNDELL.
A Student's Manual of Bibliography. [3d ed.] rev. by Roy Stokes. London: Allen and Unwin and The Library Association, 1954. 392 p.

A revision of the basic manual first published in 1932, covering the history of manuscripts and of printing (type faces, illustration, binding, collation). Two chapters deal with bibliographies and their arrangement.

"Esdaile, wisely avoiding detail, discusses the various aspects of bookmaking, collation, and description in a skilfully clear exposition. . . . In the discussion on the history of printing there is no additional material on fine printing since 1930. A list of type designers is added, but there is no mention of the recent and excellent typography at the Curwen Shakespeare Head, or the university presses. Some errors remain, others appear for the first time"—(LIBRARY JOURNAL, January, 1955, 58).

"Real errors in fact or in type are few and insignificant, and the occasional errors of dogmatism which we have noted are inevitable in such a condensed and elementary book and are more than offset by the general accuracy of statement, sanity of opinion, and clearness of exposition"—(THE LIBRARY QUARTERLY, April, 1932, 157–159).

MCKERROW, RONALD B.
An Introduction to Bibliography for Literary Students. Oxford: The Clarendon Press, 1927. 359 p.

An excellent and thorough exposition of the mechanical production of books—formats, paper, printing presses, and bibliographical techniques—from the beginning to 1800, with special emphasis upon the fifteenth and sixteenth centuries.

"The first part considers book production from the point of view of the producers, the compositor, and the pressman. The second part discusses the completed book in relation to the processes previously discussed; the final part compares the book . . . with the author's manuscript. . . . In its present enlarged state, the book will find readers among students of printing and bibliography, and will be valuable to amateur librarians and collectors"—(BOOKLIST, 24:167).

"It is not too much to say that the publication of this substantial volume is a real landmark in the development of bibliography of the critical kind"—(LONDON TIMES LITERARY SUPPLEMENT, November 3, 1927, 787).

SANDERS, CHAUNCEY.
An Introduction to Research in English Literary History: With a Chapter on Research in Folklore by Stith Thompson. New York: Macmillan, 1952. 423 p.

A manual and textbook designed as an introduction to bibliography and method for graduate students. The four major divisions are: "The Materials of Research"; "The Tools of Research"; "The Methods of Research"; and "Suggestions on Thesis-Writing." The subordinate divisions of the third section are: the problems of—editing, biography, authenticity and attribution, source study, chronology, success and influence, interpretation, technique, ideas, folklore.

"Unfortunately this valuable material is marred by the author's confused objectives and his lack of awareness of current developments in the field. He gives seven pages to book bindings and only twenty lines to cancels; he does not mention Professor Hinman's revolutionary machine for collating texts; he gives only a seven page summary to such a central subject as literary techniques, and nearly twice as many to such ancillary subjects as biography and the history of ideas. He presents in Part IV a method of documentation that has been obsolete since the MLA Style Sheet in April, 1951"—(LIBRARY JOURNAL, December, 1952, 58).

SCHNEIDER, GEORG.
Theory and History of Bibliography. New York: Columbia University Press, 1934, 306 p.

A translation by R. R. Shaw of a portion of a basic and comprehensive work, HANDBUCH DER BIBLIOGRAPHIE, first published at Leipzig in 1923, and covering, in addition to the theoretical-historical treatment (translated by Shaw) general bibliography, national bibliography, bibliographies of incunabula, newspapers, society publications, and, in addition to other data, lists of biographical dictionaries.

"It will no doubt be widely adopted as a textbook for classes in bibliography; but in this the teacher must not forget that it is, after all, only textual translation and that there is an idiom of thought as well as an idiom of language in any German writing that is not easily turned into English. If Schneider's ideas are to be assimilated by American students and his teachings adopted at their true value, the instructor will have to supply a great deal of running comment and interpretation to supplement Mr. Shaw's excellent translation"—(LIB. QUARTERLY, 5:240).

"Mr. Shaw has rendered a twofold service to American bibliographers—he has republished Schneider's treatise on the theory of their science which is no longer easily available, and he has done this in a readable English translation. . . . The scientific aspects of bibliography are quite as important as the practical. But these are matters that are not adequately treated by any of our own writers"—(LIBRARY JOURNAL, V, April, 1935).

"Written by a librarian, primarily for librarians, Schneider's discussions of the bounds, uses, and value of bibliography, as well as his consideration of more detailed matters, such as bibliographical entries and the Brussels classification, are of interest likewise, to bookmakers, scholars, and bibliographers"—(BOOKS ABROAD, VOLUME IX, 340).

SHERA, J. H. AND M. E. EGAN [EDS.].
Bibliographical Organization. Chicago: University of Chicago Press, 1951. 275 p.

A series of lectures treating of the role of bibliographic organization in contemporary civilization, the history of attempts to organize bibliography internationally, the approaches to bibliographic organization and problems, and a synthesis and summary of all that transpired at the Fifteenth annual conference of the Graduate Library School.

"The fifteenth annual conference of The Graduate Library School rendered a great service to the world of learning by assembling a group of specialists to discuss the vexing and critical problems of bibliographic organization. The papers presented before this conference now constitute, in this ably edited volume, one of the most distinguished contributions to American Library Literature. . . . The book is so charged with information and stimulative ideas that it merits careful and prolonged examination and discussion"—(THE LIBRARY QUARTERLY, XXI, 229–230).

VAN HOESEN, H. B. AND W. F. KELLER.
Bibliography, Practical, Enumerative, Historical: An Introductory Manual. New York: Scribner, 1928. 519 p.

Designed, as the "Preface" indicates, as a textbook for upperclassmen and graduate students. Aims "to indicate the scope, functions, and methods of bibliographical work of all kinds and topics," and to "describe or enumerate the fundamental works through which the student may most advantageously approach the selection of books." The basic substance of the work is adapted from a series of lectures delivered at Princeton University in 1923.

"In most cases the compilers write with first hand knowledge of the books they record, and they have supplemented their own judgment by recourse to the specialist"—(LONDON TIMES LITERARY SUPPLEMENT, September 27, 1928, 688).

"The person whose needs the authors have tried especially to keep in mind and provide for is the student, say, in the field of political science, who has begun to specialize and needs to know how to proceed in order to make a survey of the literature of his field"—(POLITICAL SCIENCE QUARTERLY, March, 1929, 124–126).

Guides and Manuals of Reference Works and Bibliographies

COLLISON, ROBERT L.
Bibliographies, Subject and National: A Guide to Their Contents, Arrangement, and Use. New York: Hafner, 1951. 172 p.

Serves as an informal bibliography of bibliographies. Part one covers subject bibliographies; part two covers national and universal bibliographies.

"A ready reference handbook, an excellent beginning text in the field. It seems essential for all reference and cataloguing collections. The compiler suggests that bibliographies make excellent reading. This one certainly does"—(LIBRARY JOURNAL, October, 1951).

"In spite of its readability and other attractive features, it is somewhat too narrowly British in point of view to serve as anything but a supplementary text in this country"—(LIBRARY QUARTERLY, April, 1952).

CROSS, TOM PEETE.
Bibliographical Guide to English Studies. Chicago: University of Chicago Press, 1947. 10th ed., with an index, 1951. 81 p.

Compiled as a guide to graduate students in the Department of English of the University of Chicago. Generally restricted to books and articles which are exclusively bibliographical or contain bibliographical features.

"A list of books and articles, chiefly bibliographical, designed to serve as an introduction to the bibliography and methods of English literary history. Librarians may find valuable suggestions as to available reference materials. Publishers are not indicated"—(BOOKLIST, XVI).

Works "such as Heyl's CURRENT NATIONAL BIBLIOGRAPHY, Baker's DRAMATIC BIBLIOGRAPHY, and Jaggard's famed (however faulty) bibliography of Shakespeare" are omitted, whereas items of lesser import, "many in periodicals" are included—(LIBRARY QUARTERLY, IX).

DOWNS, ROBERT B.
American Library Resources: A Bibliographical Guide. Chicago: American Library Association, 1951. 428 p.

A compilation of bibliographical holdings in American libraries. Approximately 6,000 titles: bibliographies, union lists, surveys, check lists, catalogs of particular libraries, special collections, whether published as separate pamphlets or books or in periodicals. In some instances, unpublished bibliographies are listed. Entries are listed according to the Dewey Decimal classification.

"This latest work is certainly his most significant contribution to the field and will be welcomed and used by research workers and librarians everywhere. . . . As the American library world becomes drawn more and more closely together through union catalogs, interlibrary centers, and other forms of inter-institutional cooperation, every facility that contributes to our knowledge of one another's resources becomes increasingly important. In this sense, Mr. Downs' new book is a significant addition to our national library structure"—(THE LIBRARY QUARTERLY, XXII, 1952, 353–354).

"Of high interest and commendably set up to date, this volume will rapidly supersede the older works and should rightfully assume its place in the library as one of the most valuable of the primary finding aids"—(UNITED STATES QUARTERLY BOOK REVIEW, VIII, 103).

ESDAILE, ARUNDELL.
The Sources of English Literature. Cambridge: Cambridge University Press, 1928. 131 p.

Contains the lectures given by the author as the Sandars Reader in Bibliography for 1926. Includes sections on: "Lists of the Works of Members of Religious Bodies"; "Bibliographies of Literary Forms"; "Lists of Bibliographies of English Literature"; "Catalogues of Private Libraries to 1887"; "Some Private Libraries"; "Booksellers and Collectors Guides."

"The ground is well covered and only specialists may perhaps complain of omissions. This is a book to be referred to rather than read. Fortunately it has an adequate index"—(NEW STATESMEN, May 26, 1928).

"Any student who reads this book carefully, and having made from it a list of all the works mentioned which concern his subject, then goes to some library which contains them and spends a few days in carefully examining them—so that he may know what they contain and in what form the information is presented—will in his knowledge of how to set about whatever piece of work he has in mind be months or even years ahead of one who has no such guide"—(ENGLISH STUDIES, May, 1928, 374–375).

GOHDES, CLARENCE.
Bibliographical Guide to the Study of the Literature of the U.S. Durham, North Carolina: Duke University Press, 1959.

A list of books designed to assist students and teachers and librarians. Does for those who are interested in the literature of the United States what guides such as those by Spargo and

Cross do for students of English literature. Special stress is given to the relationship of national literature to the literature of foreign countries.

MURPHEY, ROBERT W.
How and Where to Look It Up: A Guide to Standard Sources of Information. New York: McGraw-Hill Book Company, Inc., 1958. 721 p.

A guide to sources of information planned with the needs of the layman in mind, rather than with those of the professional librarian. Thus Part I outlines basic criteria for making an intelligent selection; explains the ways of traditional library organization; expounds some basic mechanics of research. Part II comprises an annotated list of selected sources of information.

"Only a reference librarian can appreciate fully what Robert Murphey has accomplished in this book. He has organized the more important "half of knowledge"—'Knowing where to find it'—so systematically and yet so alluringly, that libraries everywhere are bound to profit from the increased skill and hunger for knowledge that will be engendered in patrons by these pages"—("FORWARD" BY LOUIS SHORES, V).

KENNEDY, ARTHUR G.
Concise Bibliography for Students of English. Stanford University Press, 1954.

Similar to the manuals of Tom Peete Cross and John W. Spargo, but giving greater emphasis to American than to English literature. . . . a revised edition of a very fine manual, systematically arranged"—(COLLEGE ENGLISH, 1945–1946).

ROBERTS, ARTHUR D.
Introduction to Reference Books. 2d ed. London: Library Association, 1951. 214 p.

A revision of the work published in 1948, differing from it, in addition to some textual changes, in virtue of a new chapter on biographical works of reference and three short appendixes.

VITALE, PHILIP H.
An Outline Guide for English Majors. Chicago: Auxiliary University Press, 1959. 246 p.

Originally designed as a guide for graduate students in the Department of English of DePaul University. Basic contents include: list of primary readings in English and American literatures; an annotated list of selected learned journals; an annotated list of secondary readings in English and American literatures; and one hundred representative questions covering ten areas of graduate study. The "Appendix" comprises a systematic arrangement of some three hundred basic reference works.

Guides to the Use of Libraries

ALDRICH, ELLA V.
Using Books and Libraries. Englewood Cliffs, New Jersey: Prentice-Hall, Inc., 1951. 101 p.

In addition to the chapters on basic reference books, the manual contains chapters on "College and University Libraries" (the regulations and routines of the typical college or university library; "The Book" (the important parts of and the ways of intelligently using books); "Classification and Arrangement of Books" (a brief explanation of the Dewey Decimal Classification and the Library of Congress Classification systems).

HUTCHINS, MARGARET, A. S. JOHNSON, M. S. WILLIAMS.
Guide to the Use of Libraries. 3rd ed. New York: H. W. Wilson Company, 1920. 251 p.

Originally a manual for students in the University of Illinois; based upon outlines and lectures used in the presentation of actual classes in reference work. Contains nothing particularly new, but the well-known facts and principles are logically integrated and clearly explained.

"The book has a distinct purpose and a definite scope. It carries out its purpose as a class manual consistently and confines itself clearly to its scope"—(LIBRARY QUARTERLY, XLVII, November 1, 1922).

Guides to the Famous Libraries and Their Collections

BURTON, MARGARET.
Famous Libraries of the World. London: Crafton and Company, 1937. 458 p.

A companion volume to Esdaile's THE NATIONAL LIBRARIES OF THE WORLD. Among the libraries included are those of: the British Empire, France, Germany, Greece, Italy and the Vatican City, Poland, Spain, Portugal, Sweden, U.S.S.R., and the United States (specifically, Army Medical Library, Boston Public Library, Harvard University Library, Huntington Library, New York Public Library, and the Yale University Library).

For each library considered, the author conveys information relative to: foundation collection, special treasures, current acquisitions, librarians, buildings, catalogues, conditions of admission, facilities for photography, staff, finances, and library hours.

"The principle has apparently been to select libraries from as many different countries as possible. There is much to be said for this, but the result naturally is that many libraries are excluded to make room for others far less famous. . . . We have no account of the National Central Library, or of any Scottish or Welsh university, or of any modern English university, or of any Oxford or Cambridge college. Only one French, two German, and two American universities are described. No British public library is included nor any special libraries. The accounts are on the whole accurate, although there are some strange slips"—(THE LONDON TIMES LITERARY SUPPLEMENT, Aug., 1937).

"Altogether this book will prove of great value not only to libraries and members of governing bodies, but also to scholars in general"—(LIBRARY JOURNAL, November 15, 1937).

CRASTER, SIR EDMUND.
History of the Bodleian Library. Oxford: The Clarendon Press, 1952. 372 p.

Originally begun as a revision of W. C. Macrays ANNALS OF THE BODLEIAN LIBRARY, a work which first appeared in 1868. Craster however does not confine himself entirely to a chronological treatment. He divides the history of the famous library into three periods—1845–1881, 1881–1912, 1912–1945—and recounts the development of the library during each period in terms of: administration, finance, catalogues, accessions, treasures, and physical expansion.

"Though Sir Edmund reminds the reader that he has not written an official history, his book is likely to serve as a principal source of information about the Bodleian for a long time to come. Its facts are arranged according to a perspicuous plan; the difficult task of maintaining the pace of a narrative which must include hundreds of titles and consolidate a thousand details is fairly faced; and the problems of half-a-dozen librarians are presented with sympathy and understanding"—(LIBRARY QUARTERLY, October, 1953).

Directory of Libraries of the Chicago Area. Chicago: Chicago Library Club, 1945.

The publication is jointly sponsored by the Chicago Library Club and the Illinois Chapter of the Special Libraries Association. Over eight hundred private and public libraries are covered. The following is a sample entry:

MUNDELEIN COLLEGE, 1930
6353 Sheridan Road. Bri 3806
SPECIAL COLLECTIONS: Rothensteiner Collection contains some 622 rare items, including early complete folio editions of St. Augustine, St. Ambrose, St. Thomas Aquinas, St. Chrysostom, and St. Robert Bellarmine; the OLD TESTAMENT published by the Platins, 1565; and two incunabula. Library also has a third incunabulum presented by His Eminence George Cardinal Mundelein.

An invaluable directory to anyone doing scholarly research in the Chicago area.

ESDAILE, ARUNDEL.

The British Museum Library. London: George Allen and Unwin, 1946. 388 p.

The first part constitutes a historical survey; the second part constitutes an explanation of the collections and catalogs. As the author notes in the "Preface": the work is a "summary account, historical and descriptive . . . full enough to be useful for reference and information, and . . . to bring out the true significance of the collections and the tales of their gathering."

"While the book is not, and makes no claim to be, an adequate history of the library, still it is a most readable book, both useful and entertaining"—(THE LIBRARY, VOLUME 11, 1947–1948, 207).

ESDAILE, ARUNDELL.
National Libraries of the World. 2d ed. London: Library Association, 1957. 413 p.

An account of the history, administration, and public services of over thirty of the principal national libraries of the world. Each library is treated in terms of: history—foundation, collections, eminent librarians; manuscripts, buildings; catalogues; departments; staff; place in the national system; finances. A rather complete bibliography complements each chapter.

"Its only really weak section is its meagre preface of three pages in which Mr. Esdaile makes no attempt to deal with the numerous interesting problems which his book raises"—(LONDON TIMES LITERARY SUPPLEMENT, November 1, 1934).

". . . a well-timed, well-planned, well-executed and much needed book. It gives a vast amount of desired information about the library, government, organization, finances, buildings, catalogs, classifications, special services, users, librarians, staff, bibliography, and uniquely 'the place of the library in the national system' "—(LIBRARY JOURNAL, VOLUME 59, 968).

PREDEEK, ALBERT.
A History of the Libraries in Great Britain and North America. Chicago: American Library Association, 1947. 158 p.

A concise and balanced outline of the development of libraries in the British Isles and the United States from 1500 to the beginning of World War II. The work is, in fact, the author's contribution to the third volume of the HANDBUCH DER BIBLIOTHEKSWISSENSCHAFT, a monumental history of libraries.

"Leaning heavily upon secondary sources, especially the work of Edwards for the treatment of British libraries, superficially buttressed with an impressive bibliography which the author has obviously read neither wisely nor too well, and filled with errors of fact and interpretation, these chapters contribute nothing to existing knowledge of library history in either Great Britain or the United States. This is especially unfortunate since the reputation of the HANDBUCH wili add to the treatment an authenticity, at least with librarians, that it does not deserve"—(LIBRARY QUARTERLY, July, 1948).

Standard Catalog for Public Libraries: An Annotated List of 12,300 Titles with a Full Analytical Index. New York: Wilson, 1950. 2057 p.

The main part of the work comprises a list of books which the average public library or medium-sized library will be able to afford and find most useful. A secondary part comprises an author, title, subject, and analytical index which, in addition to indexing all the titles in the main part contains analytical entries to parts of some 2,000 books. Comment, sometimes fairly extensive, more often brief, are given for virtually all the titles. Kept up by supplements issued annually and cumulating at intervals.

"A classified list, completely indexed, exceedingly useful"—(THE BOOKLIST, XXXI, January, 1935, 175).

"The analytical index that takes up 650 of the nearly 2,000 pages of the work is a masterpiece of modern indexing"—(BOOK REVIEW DIGEST, 1935).

THOMPSON, JAMES.
The Ancient Library. Chicago: College and Research Libraries, 1941. 120 p.

A lucid and organic, but rather sketchy account of the libraries of the East, of Rome and Greece.

"It is too brief for its theme. Fifty pages attempt to summarize our knowledge of Egyptian, Mesopotamian, Greek, and Roman libraries. Forty-eight pages discuss various technical matters, e.i., format of books, library architecture, cataloging and classification, administration, book production and bookselling throughout the whole ancient period. . . . On the one hand it is over-journalistic; on the other hand, over-erudite.

. . . The book is not a satisfactory contribution to the historical literature of librarianship. Treatment of Egyptian and Mesopotanian libraries is inadequate and sometimes inaccurate. . . . In spite of imperfections every historical library should have a copy. . . . Professor Thompson makes comparisons, gives suggestions and opens perspectives which will help later compilers of the same subject"—(THOUGHT, VOLUME 16, June, 1941).

THOMPSON, JAMES W.
The Medieval Library. Chicago: University of Chicago Press, 1939. 661 p.

A comprehensive, scholarly, and very readable account of the libraries in the Middle Ages, the four parts being: (1) The Early Middle Ages (2) The High Middle Ages (3) The Close of the Middle Ages and the Italian Renaissance (4) The Making and Care of the Book in the Middle Ages. Contains no bibliography, but copious footnotes—some 2,228 of them—are scattered throughout the work.

"For lovers of books and students of culture, Professor's work is a chest of buried treasure"—(CHRISTIAN CENTURY, August 30, 1939).

". . . if it were later found practical to publish a supplement containing a general index and bibliography, every reader of the book—and over the years in which this volume will remain useful, they will be many—would be grateful"—(SATURDAY REVIEW OF LITERATURE, December 23, 1939).

"The chapter on Jewish and Moslem Libraries might have been extended considerably by consulting G. Sartois' works more thoroughly. What is said on Egyptian monastic libraries is quite inadequate, misleading, and all but useless"—(CATHOLIC WORLD, March, 1940, 112–114).

Bibliographies of Bibliographies

BESTERMAN, THEODORE.
A World Bibliography of Bibliographies and of Bibliographical Catalogues, Calendars, Abstracts, Digests, Indexes, and the

Like. 2d ed. rev. and greatly enlarged throughout. London: priv. pub. by the author, 1947–49. 3 vols. 3d and final ed. Geneva: Societas Bibliographica, 1954–1956. 4 vols.

A classified list of some 80,000 separately published bibliographies, including lists of archive materials, calendars, as well as lists of abridgements of patent specifications issued by the patent offices. The specific aim of the work was to bring up to date Petzholdt's BIBLIOTHECA BIBLIOGRAPHICA.

"Bibliography cannot be an art for its own sake; its merits must be judged solely by the standards of its usefulness for a definite purpose. I am afraid that the actual use of the WORLD BIBLIOGRAPHY will by no means be commensurate with the immense labor involved in its compilation"—(PAPERS OF THE BIBLIOGRAPHICAL SOCIETY OF AMERICA, VOLUME 36, 1942, 321–324).

Bibliographical Index: A Cumulative Bibliography of Bibliographies, 1937–. New York: Wilson, 1938–. Volume 1, 1937–1942 (published in 1945), 1780 p.; Volume II, 1943–1946 (published in 1948), 831 p.

An extensive and useful list of separately published bibliographies and bibliographies included in books and periodicals (as many as 1,500 being examined regularly). The arrangement is alphabetical by subject only.

"The librarian expects a bibliography to perform a service similar to that of the library catalog, only on a broader basis, since it is not limited to the contents of one library and includes "analytical" entries of articles in periodicals, of parts of books, etc., as very few library catalogs do at all extensively. The BIBLIOGRAPHICAL INDEX cuts the scope in two in that it 'locates' material by subject only and not by author. . . . A bibliography arranged under detailed 'specific subject' entries, supplemented by no classified arrangement, and with no author index, thus functions in only one of the three ways of the library catalog"—(LIBRARY QUARTERLY, April, 1940, 272–274).

"The quality of Mr. Besterman's work, his scrupulous care over detail, and his own vast knowledge of the field would indicate to this reviewer the quality of the work; one need only read the preface to realize how much thought and care have gone into it"—DOCUMENTATION, March, 1956, 44).

CONOVER, Helen F.

Current National Bibliographies. Washington: U.S. Library of Congress, 1955. 132 p.

Supersedes the listings published in preliminary form in the Library of Congress Quarterly Journal of Current Acquisitions, first accumulated in 1950, and the Supplement covering February 1950 through November 1952. In addition to the regular records of the book trade, the annotated lists include periodical indexes, government publications, and directories of periodicals and newspapers.

COURTNEY, William P.

Register of National Bibliography: With a Selection of the Chief Bibliographical Books and Articles Printed in Other Countries. London: Constable, 1905–1912. 3 Volumes. 631 p.

Volumes I and II comprise a list of bibliographies published before 1905; volume three comprises a supplement containing about 10,000 additional references principally to bibliographies published 1905–1912. All of the items are listed alphabetically over the span of the three volumes. Each volume is indexed; the third volume contains an appendix which includes materials not included in Volume I and Volume II. Each page is divided into two columns with the first and last captions of the page listed at the top of the column for ready reference.

"This work possesses the exactness and the completeness which was to be expected of the joint-compiler of the BIBLIOTHECA CORNUBIENSIS and contributor to the D.N.B. It includes references not only to separate bibliographical monographs, but also to such lists as are to be found in periodicals and other works—after the manner of Mr. Whitney's most useful catalog of bibliographies. Moreover, it comprises references not simply to those works which are also to be found only in the largest libraries, but also to those popular lists which are to be found in every library"—(LIBRARY JOURNAL, VOLUME 30, 426–427).

"An admirable volume by a master of the subject. Such careful and thorough work will be properly valued by all experts"—(ATHENAEUM, March 23, 1912, 338).

"Useful it certainly is, with its wealth of information, especially on the minutiae of bibliography and on material buried in out-of-the-way places. But one cannot help thinking how much more useful it would have been if more care had been exercised in its preparation, and if Mr. Courtney had confined his efforts, as was originally his intention, to English bibliography"—(THE NATION, 81, 365).

HEYL, LAWRENCE.
Current National Bibliographies. A List of Sources of Information Concerning Current Books of all Countries. Rev. ed. Chicago: American Library Association, 1942. 20 p.

Lists sources of information concerning the books of sixty-two countries. Arranges material alphabetically according to country. Has no index; but the list is so brief that the lack of an index makes for no serious hardship.

NORTHUP, CLARK S.
Register of Bibliographies of the English Language and Literature. New Haven: Yale University Press, 1925. 507 p.

Includes many related bibliographies of other subjects and hence serves to a degree as a general bibliography of bibliography. The main divisions of the work are: I (general, 9–33); II (individual authors and topics, 34–417); additions and corrections (419–449); index (451–507).

"A new bibliography of literary bibliographies, the importance of which in a college or reference library it would be difficult to over-estimate. . . . All entries are given with exact reference, there are some critical and descriptive notes, and reference to reviews is made"—(LIBRARY JOURNAL, January 15, 1926).

"This very substantial dictionary of bibliographies of English authors and of works bearing on English literature contains about 10,000 entries, and is a good example of the laborious thoroughness of the present-day school of American bibliographers"—(LIBRARY ASSOCIATION RECORD, VOLUME 4, NUMBER 28, 143).

JOSEPHSON, A. G. S.
Bibliographies of Bibliographies: Chronologically Arranged, with Occasional Notes and An Index. Chicago: Bibliographical Society of Chicago, 1901. 45 p.

The first edition is a chronological list of 156 bibliographies of bibliographies. In a second edition, the compiler replaced the chronological arrangement by a classified arrangement, within which he arranges the titles chronologically.

"About two-thirds of the titles cataloged have been personally examined by the author. . . . This little list, with the help of the very full author and subject index supplies an excellent key to sources of information which cannot be readily found elsewhere"—(LIBRARY JOURNAL, April, 1901, 578).

VAN PATTEN, NATHAN.
Index to Bibliographies and Bibliographical Contributions Relating to the World of American and British Authors, 1923–1932. California: Stanford University Press, 1934. 507 p.

Aims to make more accessible information regarding the printed and manuscript work of individual authors—binding, paper, pagination, illustration, variants, editions, issues, value, and location. Chronologically, continues the work of Northup's REGISTER.

". . . the compiler has covered a wide field, and assembled a mass of useful information, otherwise difficult to obtain, in a conveniently small compass"—(LONDON TIMES LITERARY SUPPLEMENT, May, 1934).

Universal Bibliographies

PEDDIE, ROBERT A.
Subject Index of Books Published Before 1800. London: Grafton, 1933–.

The first series, 745 p., was published in 1933; the second series, 857 p., was published in 1935; the third series, 945 p., was published in 1939; and the last series, 872 p., appeared in 1948.

Each issue constitutes an alphabetical subject list of some 50,000 books in many languages, published before 1800. The third series includes in its alphabetical arrangement all the headings employed in the three series with cross references to the first and second series. The last series does not continue this record.

WATT, ROBERT.
Bibliotheca Britannica: Or a General Index to British and Foreign Literature. Edinburgh: Constable, 1824. 4 vols.

Volumes one and two contain authors and their works; volumes three and four contain subjects that have been written about. Includes British authors and authors whose works have been translated into English.

More fully, Volumes I and II comprise an alphabetical list of authors and their works, providing full name and dates, brief biographical data, and, for each book, brief information which generally includes title, date, size, and number of volumes. Volumes III and IV constitute a chronological arrangement of the subject headings, with the references being made, not to the author, but to the page and marginal index letter in the author volumes where the full entry is to be found.

"This is a very useful work; a must for every library"—(BLACKWOOD'S MAGAZINE REVIEW, 553).

"On the whole, it seems to us that all those who prize the honour of British literature, will do well to contribute, as far as in them lies, to the success of this admirable book. . . . for it is quite impossible that the time consumed on the BIBLIOTHECA BRITANNICA should ever be adequately paid for in the usual routine of the trade"—(BLACKWOOD'S EDINBURGH MAGAZINE, August, 1819, 555).

International Bibliographies

BALDENSPERGER, F. AND W. FRIEDERICH.
Bibliography of Comparative Literature. Chapel Hill: University of North Carolina Press, 1950. 701 p.

A comprehensive bibliography. The first and third books deal with generalities—themes, motifs, genres, international literary relations; the second and fourth, with specific literatures and their contributions—of one country on another, of one author on another, then the influence of a country on an individual author. The bibliographical citations are brief, the table of contents is quite detailed, but the index is lacking.

"It is the most comprehensive and effective tool ever placed in the hands of comparatists, and should for many years to come do much to center attention on comparative literature. It is excellently printed, clear and readable, firmly bound for every duty, and accurate. It is an almost superhuman task of painstaking scholarship"—(GERMANIC REVIEW, XXVI, 165–166).

The work makes available to students of literature "an invaluable, indispensable tool, an up-to-date, very full, and generally accurate survey of all scholarship which can be called comparative literature. . . . The arrangement, which repeats Betz's scheme with some modifications, seems lucid and logical, once one has grasped the main principle that always the 'emitter' of an influence is the guide for the listing. . . . A weak section is that on the main literary genres. . . . The section on the novel is particularly defective. . . . The list of the general works on literary criticism is also quite small and defective. . . . The part on 'Literature and Politics,' which opens with a chapter on sociology and lists Marxism expressly among its topics, is possibly even more deficient. . . . . A second major deficiency of the work is the step—motherly treatment of Slavic matters. . . . The work could be made nearly perfect by small corrections, if substantially supplemented in the two directions I have indicated—literary theory and Slavic titles"—(COMPARATIVE LITERATURE, VOLUME 3, 90–92).

EDWARDES, MARIAN.
Summary of the Literatures of Modern Europe (England, France, Germany, Italy, Spain) From the Origins to 1400.
London: Dent, 1907. 352 p.

An annotated and classified bibliography with references to most authoritative scholarly discussions of the writings included. Major arrangement is by countries; subordinate arrangement is by principal writers. Provides brief biographical data, list of works, notes about works, and bibliographical references to editions, translations, and critical works and articles. Manuscripts in various English libraries are located.

"Such a book . . . is not likely to appeal to any but professional students, and this class of readers will surely prefer to go at once to the sources for the individual literatures which Miss Edwardes herself has used, rather than consult them at second hand in the present work. . . . We have no space to record the innumerable omissions and errors which we have observed in the English Literature division of this work. . . . It is no better with the sections on French Literature. . . . But enough has been said, we believe, to show how defective this work is, notwithstanding its occasionally useful citations of recent literature"—(THE NATION, VOLUME 85, November 21, 1907, 424).

"It seems a very careful and painstaking work, and should be found useful by students"—(THE SPECTATOR, March 16, 1907, 469–470).

In spite of certain defects "the compilation is distinctly serviceable. With careful revision it might be made indispensable"—(ATHENAEUM, VOLUME 1, June 29, 1907, 789).

FARRAR, C. P., A. P. EVANS.
A Bibliography of English Translations From Medieval Sources.
New York: Columbia University Press, 1946. 643 p.

Compiled in response to a demand for a reasonable, accurate guide to existing translations from medieval sources. Official papers are excluded; the aim is to "include English translations of important literary sources from Constantine the Great to the year 1500 within an area roughly inclusive of Europe, North Africa, and West Asia, generally." Most translations from Latin are excluded. Arrangement is alphabetical, chiefly by author. Each separate item is numbered. Annotations describe content, convey translator's comment. Contains an extensive index to authors, translators, editors, titles, subjects.

"This bibliography fills a critical need at a critical time; it reflects scholarship of the highest sort, and on every page shows the industry, patience, and skill of all who aided in its production. . . . Students and scholars can rejoice in the possession of a work on which they will all lean heavily, and librarians should consider themselves thrice blest to have such an aid at hand"—(AMERICAN HISTORICAL REVIEW, LII, 1946, 108).

"Fills a great need and will prove an invaluable tool for all students of the medieval period. . . . An excellent index, over seventy pages in length, and adequate cross references will please the many future users"—(UNITED STATES QUARTERLY BOOKLIST, 11, 1946, 260).

HOPPER, V. F. and B. N. GREBANIER.
Bibliography of European Literature. New York: Barron's Educational Series, Inc., 1954. 158 p.

Conceived as a companion to the authors' ESSENTIALS OF EUROPEAN LITERATURE, this bibliography is limited to books in English on the subjects covered in the companion volume: the leading writers and their works, the key periods and literary productions, minor figures, national literatures in general.

"It appears that not all English translations, or even the best, are necessarily listed. But in spite of this inadequacy, it does make available in a small, inexpensive volume, a guide for the study of European literature in translation and, with the authors, we may hope that it 'will encourage a vaster work on the subject' "—(WILSON LIBRARY BULLETIN, XXIX, September, 1954, 85).

STILLWELL, MARGARET B.
Incunabula and Americana, 1450–1800. Key to Bibliographical Study. New York: Columbia University Press, 1931. 483 p.

Lists 35,232 copies of 11,132 titles owned by 332 public and 390 private collections. In part one, Incunabula, the contents are: (ch. 1) printed books of the 15th century; (ch. 2) identification and collation; (ch. 3) bibliographical reference material. In part two, Americana, the contents are: (ch. 1) preliminary survey of sources and methods; (ch. 2) century of maritime discovery; (ch. 3) two centuries of colonial growth; (ch. 4) later Americana and the Revolutionary periods; (ch. 5) early printing in America. The Reference Sections contain: (1) notes and definitions; (2) foreign bibliographical terms; (3) Latin contractions and abbreviations; (4) placenames of 15th century printing towns; (5) Bibliography—some 1,300 items.

"Altogether, the work seems admirably adequate to its purpose and sets a high standard . . ."—(TRANSACTIONS OF THE BIBLIOGRAPHICAL SOCIETY, VOLUME 22, 4).

U.S. Library of Congress: A Catalog of Books Representing Library of Congress Printed Cards, issued to July 31, 1942. Ann Arbor, Michigan: Edward Bros., 1942–1946. 167 v.

An author and main entry catalog of books for which Library of Congress Cards have been printed in the Library of Congress, the many government department libraries, or the various libraries throughout the nation that take part in the cooperative cataloguing program.

U.S. Library of Congress Author Catalog: A Cumulative List of Works Represented by Library of Congress Printed Cards, 1948–1952. Ann Arbor, Michigan: J. W. Edwards, 1953.

Sometimes called the Cumulative Catalog of Library of Congress Printed Cards. Contains not only main entries, but also essential entries and cross references. Volumes 1–23, Authors, A–Z; volume 24, Films. Many cards represented in these volumes were prepared by cooperating libraries, so that for a large number of books not in the Library of Congress at least one location is indicated. Starting with January, 1953, entries are listed separately for Motion Pictures and filmstrips, music and phonorecords.

U.S. Library of Congress Catalog: A Cumulative List of Works Represented by Library of Congress Printed Cards. Books, Subjects, 1950–1954. Ann Arbor, Michigan: J. W. Edwards, 1955. 20 v.

Motion pictures and music scores are included through 1952, but are listed separately since January, 1953. As is the case with the Author section, many of the cards were prepared by cooperating libraries; so that for many books not in the Library of Congress, at least one location is indicated.

National Bibliographies

American Catalogue of Books, 1876–1910. New York: Publisher's Weekly, 1876–1910. 9 v. in 13.

The 1938 reprint is a continuation of BIBLIOTHECA AMERICANA, compiled by Roorbach, the fourth volume of which brought the work down to 1861. The 1941 reprint under the direction of F. Leypoldt in 1880 was compiled by Lynds E. Jones and published by Peter Smith in 1941.

The aim of the work is to include, with certain exceptions, all the books published in the United States which were in print and for sale to the general public on July 1, 1876. The exceptions to this are: local directories, periodicals, sheet music, books chiefly blank, unbound maps, tracts, and other low-priced pamphlets. Entries number 70,000 and represent the work of over 900 firms.

"On behalf of bibliographers and reference workers, this department wishes to pay tribute to Peter Smith and the National Bibliophile Service. From time to time his concern has rendered librarianship and the world of scholarship signal service, both in the location of rare and out of print items and in the reprinting of needed standard works . . . and now comes a most welcome P.S. from Peter Smith: 'We hope to announce shortly our project for a reprint of the AMERICAN CATALOGUE OF BOOKS, 1876–1910 (the whole blessed business)'"—(WILSON LIBRARY BULLETIN, VOL. XIII, 482).

Annual American Catalogue, 1886–1910. New York: Publisher's Weekly, 1887–1911. 25 v.

Directly based upon Publisher's Weekly's cumulated reference lists as preserved by the linotype system, edited and filled out with additional titles brought to notice during the years of publication. Discontinued for lack of support, and now generally superseded by the cumulated volumes of the AMERICAN CATALOGUE, but useful for occasional omissions in the AMERICAN CATALOGUE.

Books in Print: An Author-Title-Series Index to the Publishers' Trade List Annual, 1948—. New York: Bowker, 1948—.

Provides full information concerning author, title, price, publisher, and thus makes possible easy reference to the appropriate catalogue in the Trade List Annual. One alphabet lists authors, editions, compilers, and translators; the other alphabet lists titles, series, and serial publications. Both indexes give bibliographical information.

"The British book trade has long had a toll similar to this index, namely WHITAKER'S REFERENCE CATALOGUE OF CURRENT LITERATURE. American bookstores and libraries have not had any index of books in print since the 1928 volume of the U.S. CATALOG. The major aim of the volume is to provide in a single volume enough information to enable the vast majority of bookseller's inquiries to be turned into orders"—(LIBRARY JOURNAL, April 1948).

British National Bibliography, No. 1, Jan. 4, 1950. London: Council of the British National Bibliography, British Museum, 1950.

A weekly bibliography of books published in Great Britain, compiled by highly trained cataloguers, working on the books themselves as they pass through the copyright Receipt Office at the British Museum. The descriptions are precise and adequate; the subjects are defined and analyzed with clarity. The classified subject section takes up the first 686 pages; the author, title, and subject index takes up the remaining 268 pages. The cataloguing includes: full name of author, title, publisher, date, pagination, illustration, cm. size, binding, series, occasional annotations.

"A careful sampling has produced only a handful of trivial slips, so few that they merely confirm its substantial accuracy. The index is as nearly perfect an instrument as could be contrived. . . . The British National Bibliography has already established itself as a necessary companion in every bookshop and library where English books are to be found"—(LONDON TIMES LITERARY SUPPLEMENT, July 4, 1952).

"The publication reflects the greatest credit on everyone concerned with it, to whom our warmest congratulations are due"—(LIBRARY ASSOCIATION RECORD, XVII, April, 1950).

Cumulative Book Index. New York: Wilson, 1998—. Service Basis.

Aims to catalogue all the books in the English language wherever published, and thus to form a complete bibliography of works in English, exclusive of government documents, tracts, propaganda, and issues of very local or ephemeral nature. Published periodically with cumulation to form supplements to the UNITED STATES CATALOG.

"A comprehensive and reasonably accurate record indispensable in any library."

EVANS, CHARLES.

American Bibliography: A Chronological Dictionary of all Books, Pamphlets, and Periodical Publications Printed in the United States of America from the Genesis of Printing in 1639 down to and Including the Year 1820; with Bibliographical and Biographical Notes. Chicago: Privately printed for the author by the Columbia Press, 1903–1934. Vol. 1–12.

The first volume was published in 1903, the twelfth and last volume, covering the years 1798–1799, was published in 1934, just one year before Evans' death. A reprint was made in 1941–42 by Peter Smith, New York.

Each book lists author's full name, with dates of birth and death, full title, publication facts, and, in many instances, location. Each volume contains an author index, a subject index, and a publisher or printer index.

"For ten years the AMERICAN BIBLIOGRAPHY has been in practical use, both in this country and abroad, and is recognized everywhere as the bibliographical authority of early American literature" – (LIBRARY JOURNAL, XXXVIII, 46–47).

"The only serious criticism one can make of his plan, is that he never gives any authorities for borrowed information. It is taken as it is found, good, bad or indifferent, and its source is never credited. The taint of uncertainty or unreliability which belongs to titles of this class thus pervades to a certain extent the whole work, and one is not always able to tell whether Mr. Evans has seen the book or has taken the title for an uncertain source" – (LIBRARY JOURNAL, XXXIV, March, 134).

The American Bibliography of Charles Evans: A Chronological Dictionary of All Books, Pamphlets and Periodical Publications Printed in the United States of America from the genesis of printing in 1639 down to and including the year 1800 with bibliographical and biographical notes. Volume 13, 1799–1800, by Clifford K. Shipton. Worcester, Massachusetts: American Antiquarian Society, 1955. 349 p.

A continuation of Charles Evans' AMERICAN BIBLIOGRAPHY, which ended with the letter M for 1799. Shipton's volume starts with the letter N for 1799 and continues through 1800, with author and subject indexes. Titles are shortened and symbols for location adapted. Cross references are given for anonymous works listed under author.

KELLEY, JAMES.
American Catalogue of Books Published in the United States from January 1861 to January 1871. New York: Wiley, 1866–1871. 2 v.

A continuation of Roorbach's BIBLIOTHECA AMERICANA and, like the latter, neither complete nor entirely accurate. Yet the BIBLIOTHECA AMERICANA and the AMERICAN CATALOGUE OF BOOKS are the most general lists available for the period 1820–1870.

ROORBACH, ORVILLE AUGUSTUS.
Bibliotheca Americana, 1820–1861. New York: Roorbach, 1852–61. 4 v.

An alphabetical list of American publications, including reprints. Arrangement is by author and title; gives publication facts, size and price.

"Roorbach, although his work is most imperfect bibliographically, is entitled to credit for his personal labors and professional enterprise in making the first real American Catalogue" – (LIBRARY JOURNAL, August, 1897, 387).

SABIN, JOSEPH.
Dictionary of Books Relating to America from its Discovery to the Present Time. New York: Bibliographical Society of America, 1928–1936. 29 v.

The actual number of entries probably exceed 107,000. The principal plan of arrangement is by author. The facts given include: full title, publication facts, often contents and bibliographical notes with reference to a review in some other work, and, occasionally, location.

"Joseph Sabin's great Dictionary . . . was left incomplete on his death in 1881, when 82 parts, bringing the work into its fourteenth volume, had been put through the press. . . . A truly monumental work"—(LIBRARY JOURNAL, January, 1924, 84).

United States Catalog: Books in Print, 1899. Minneapolis: The H. W. Wilson Company, 1900. 2 v. in 1.

Each volume alphabetically lists entries under author, title, and subject. Whereas the first edition, however, contained separate author and title indexes, the succeeding editions have grouped author, title, and subject in a single alphabet. And whereas the first three editions excluded books published outside the United States, the fourth edition includes Canadian and British publications, privately printed books, and the publications of universities, societies, scientific institutions, as well as a selected list of the publications of the national and state government.

The UNITED STATES CATALOG, together with its supplements and related publication, the CUMULATIVE INDEX, makes available the most complete record of book publishing in America since 1898.

United States Copyright Office: Catalog of Entries, 1891–1946. Washington, D.C. The Government Printing Office, 1891–1947.

The arrangement and format have varied with different issues. With the third series, published in 1947, the Catalog was subdivided into separate parts following the classification noted in the Copyright Act: pt. 1A, Books and Selected Pamphlets; pt. 1B, Pamphlets, Serials, and Contributions to Periodicals; pt. 3 and 4, Dramas and Works Prepared for Oral Delivery; pt. 5A, Published Music; pt. 5B, Unpublished Music; pt. 6, Maps; pt. 7–11B, Works of Art, Reproduction, Prints; pt. 12 and 13, Motion Pictures; pt. 14A, Renewal Registrations, Literature, Art, Film; pt. 14B, Renewal Registrations, Music.

The book sections includes books published in the United States, books in foreign languages published abroad, and books in the English language first published abroad when they are copyrighted in this country.

U.S. Library of Congress. The National Union Catalog: A Cumulative Author List Representing Library of Congress Printed Cards and Titles Reported by Other American Libraries. Compiled by the Library of Congress with the cooperation of the Committee on Resources of American Libraries of the American Library Association. Ann Arbor, Michigan: Edwards, 1958. 28 vols.

Since January, 1956, it has included titles catalogued and holdings reported by some 500 libraries. From January to June, 1956, monthly and quarterly issues had the title: LIBRARY OF CONGRESS CATALOG-BOOKS: Authors; a National Union Catalog Representing Library of Congress Printed Cards and Titles Reported by Other Libraries. In July, 1956, the title changed to THE NATIONAL UNION CATALOG. Symbols are used to indicate copies held by other libraries.

General Bibliographies

American Library Association Catalog: An annotated Basic List of 10,000 Books. Chicago: American Library Association, 1926–.

The 1926 issue, 1,295 pages, covers approximately 10,000 books. It is a classified list, generally following the Dewey Decimal System, which provides the following information for each entry: author, title, date, paging, publishers, price, Library of Congress card number, and an indication of scope and value.

The second issue of the A.L.A. CATALOGUE covers some 3,000 titles appearing in the years 1926–1931 (1930, 340 p.); the third issue covers about 4,000 titles appearing in the years 1932–1936 (1938, 306 p.); the fourth issue covers about 4,000 titles appearing in the years 1937–1941 (1943, 306 p.); the fifth issue covers about 4,500 titles appearing in the years 1942–1949 (1952, 408 p.).

Lists only works published in the United States; does provide annotations from other comments, but without an indication of the source.

"The biography section is a treasure house of good reading. It is impossible to criticize it"—(LIBRARY JOURNAL, LXI, 1081).

"The policy of using notes without giving credit seems a dubious one; yet withal, the ALA CATALOG . . . is certainly a very useful tool, and everyone connected with its fashioning should have the gratitude of the profession"—(LITERARY QUARTERLY, XII, 1120).

Booklist: A Guide to Current Books, 1905—. Chicago: American Library Association, 1905—.

Issued semimonthly September through July—the single August issue being the volume index. Information given includes: author's full name, title, date, paging, publisher, price, Dewey decimal classification number, and a brief description of the basic contents of the book, its general value, and an indication of the type of library for which it is recommended.

The Booklist and Subscription Books Bulletin. Chicago: American Library Association, 1956—.

A combination of THE BOOKLIST and the SUBSCRIPTION BOOKS BULLETIN. The reviews of the Subscription Books Committee are published in the first pages of THE BOOKLIST, but are not separately paged. Generally reviews fewer books per year than the old SUBSCRIPTION BOOKS BULLETIN.

HOFFMAN, HESTER R.
Bookman's Manual: A Guide to Literature. 8th ed. New York: R. R. Bowker Company, 1958. 987 p.

Covers many fields—the humanities, reference works, science, travel, the book trade, and generally provides brief though useful annotations. This revised and enlarged edition includes two chapters which have been almost completely rewritten. "The new chapter on Greek and Roman Classics in Translation has replaced the old chapter on Classics in Translation. The classics in other foreign languages which formerly had a place here . . .

have been transferred to the new and greatly augmented chapter on Other Foreign Literature."

GRACE, SISTER M. AND G. C. PETERSON.
Books for Catholic Colleges: A Supplement to Shaw's LIST OF BOOKS FOR COLLEGE LIBRARIES. Compiled under the auspices of the Catholic Library Association. Chicago: American Library Association, 1948. 134 p.

"This book deserves a far greater appreciation than either its appearance or title warrants . . . but for the seven pages on religion, the book is a universal tool. . . . All the books listed, with very few exceptions, are in print, the LC number is given, where it is available, and as a selective list of the best of books in the fields of the humanities, literature, and elementary science, it cannot fail to be an aid"—(LIBRARY JOURNAL).

SHAW, CHARLES B.
A List of Books for College Libraries: Approximately 14,000 Titles Selected on the Recommendation of 200 College Teachers, Librarians, and Other Advisers. Chicago: American Library Association, 1931. 810 p.

A basic list, with twenty-four major divisions and an author index. The 1931–1938 edition (1940, 284 p.) omits titles published within the period which were definitely regarded as out-of-print. References to book reviews are often given.

Standard Catalog for Public Libraries. 3d ed. New York: The H. W. Wilson Company, 1950. 2057 p.

The main alphabet covers 12,300 titles of books, pamphlets, periodicals, and other publications particularly suitable for small or medium sized public libraries. In addition there are 3,555 titles listed in the notes, including specialized and out-of-print items. Annotations are given for all titles and many editions; preferred items are starred; the Dewey decimal class numbers, subject headings, and Library of Congress card numbers are included.

Subscription Books Bulletin. Chicago: American Library Association, 1930—.

Devoted exclusively to reviews of reference works—encyclopedias, dictionaries, biographical works, atlases, collections, etc. Published as a quarterly from 1930 to September, 1956, when it was combined with the BOOKLIST and began to appear as THE BOOKLIST-SUBSCRIPTION BOOKS BULLETIN. Lists are classified generally: books suitable for smaller libraries; books suitable for children; lists of government publications, etc. Both the Dewey decimal numbers and the Library of Congress classification numbers are given for each publication.

United States Quarterly Book List. New Brunswick, New Jersey: Rutgers University Press, 1945–1956.

Provides a bibliographical description, in Library of Congress form, with a description of general contents and, whenever possible, a biographical sketch of the author. Covers mainly such areas as: fine arts, literature, philosophy and religion, biography, the social sciences, the biological sciences, the physical sciences, technology, and reference.

English Literature Bibliographies

GENERAL

Cambridge Bibliography of English Literature. F. W. Bateson, ed. New York: The Macmillan Company, 1941. 4 vols.

An extensive, comprehensive, and scholarly bibliography, the standard in its field. Supersedes the bibliographies listed in the CHEL and is supplemented by the works of the MHRA and the CBEL supplement. Fully records newspapers and magazines, as well as books and learned periodicals. Major arrangement is by periods; subordinate arrangement is by literary forms or general topics and by authors. For each author generally gives: bibliographies of the author; collected editions of his works; separate works; biographical and critical works about the author. The bibliographies appear in the first three volumes; a detailed index constitutes the fourth volume.

"The CBEL is a scholar's bibliography compiled by scholars who understand the uses which other scholars will make of it." —(AMERICAN LITERATURE, XIII, 183–184).

"What is impressive in this new bibliography of English Literature is the scope of the undertaking. It will be useful to students of religion, of philosophy, of education, of political and social conditions, of the history of science. . . . The CBEL is more than a catalogue. It is, in addition, a short-hand history of English Literature"—(JOURNAL OF ENGLISH PHILOLOGY, 40, 1941, 464).

"If a work of reference does not function smoothly in its capacity as a machine for answering questions, then certainly it is of little worth. On this score the new Cambridge bibliography is about as useful as anything that exists. Certainly every college and university library will be incomplete without it"—(COMMONWEAL, 33, 568).

Cambridge Bibliography of English Literature, F. W. Bateson, ed. Vol. 5, Supplement: A.D. 600–1900, George Watson, ed. New York: Cambridge University Press, 1957. 710 p.

The Supplement lists publications of scholarly interest down to 1900 which have appeared since the original bibliography was prepared in 1941. "As nearly as possible sections have been brought down to the beginning of the year 1955."

WATSON, GEORGE.

Concise Cambridge Bibliography of English Literature, 600–1950. New York: Cambridge University Press, 1958. 271 p.

A condensed treatment of some 400 "major" authors, selected from the CBEL and its Supplement, with the addition of a section covering 1900–1950. The six chronological sections are preceded by a general introductory section providing bibliographies, literary history and criticism, collections, dictionaries, etc. The bibliographies include both primary and secondary works.

KENNEDY, ARTHUR G.

A Bibliography of the Writings on the English Language from the Beginnings of Printing to the End of 1922. Cambridge: Harvard University Press, 1927. 517 p.

Aims to provide students of English with a simple but complete book of reference, and to assist those students who seek to specialize in the history of linguistics. Covers both language and literature, and is classified with indexes to authors and reviewers and to subjects.

"This is without a doubt the most important contribution of recent years within the field of English Language. It is the result of some fourteen years of research and more than 15,000 volumes of serial publications have been checked. With its 13,402 items, the volume is offered as a complete book of reference on the subject of the scientific study of England; books dealing with the artistic aspect, literary style, art of expression, have been omitted, unless they emphasize questions of grammatical usage . . ."—(FEGP, XXVII, 1928, 437–440).

"One section of the book lends itself to considerable comment, that on slang and colloquialisms. This stops at 1900 and so the period of the Great War is ruled out. . . . French and German works are referred to and quoted. It is indeed quite a complete bibliography"—(LONDON TIMES LITERARY SUPPLEMENT, June 16, 1927, 428).

OLD AND MIDDLE ENGLISH

GENERAL

FARRAR, CLARISSA P., A. PATERSON.
Bibliography of English Translations from Medieval Sources. New York: Columbia University Press, 1946, 534 p.

For annotation, see page 217.

HEUSINKVELD, A. H. AND E. J. BASHE.
A Bibliographical Guide to Old English: A Selective Bibliography of the Language, Literature, and History of the Anglo-Saxons. Iowa City: University of Iowa Press, 1931. 153 p.

Aims to assist student by (1) providing him with "a guide to the bibliographical tools most likely to prove necessary and useful" in a more than superficial study of old English; (2) reminding him that "language and literature are but two of many phenomena in the Anglo-Saxon period"; and (3) providing him with "a list of the most important literary and linguistic monuments" of the period.

". . . fills up far more completely than the authors' modesty will admit a serious gap which has long existed in the equipment of tools at the disposal of students and readers. It is about as complete as the first edition of a work of this sort could reasonably expect to be; it is intelligently and conveniently arranged; it is well-indexed; it is selective yet almost certainly fulfills the authors' hopes 'that the material actually will lead the student to all other works that have been deliberately or inadvertently omitted' " — (SPECULUM, VII, 287).

LOOMIS, ROGER S.
Introduction to Medieval Literature Chiefly in England: A Reading List and Bibliography. 2d ed. New York: Columbia University Press, 1948. 32 p.

"The ten years which have elapsed since the first appearance of Professor Loomis' unassuming but worthwhile syllabus have brought forth no rivals. Revision has allowed the author to keep abreast of the thriving course of medieval scholarship during the decade" — (MODERN LANGUAGE QUARTERLY, March, 1950, 498).

MUMMENDEY, RICHARD.
Language and Literature of the Anglo-Saxon Nations as Presented in German Doctoral Dissertations, 1885–1950: A Bibliography. Charlottesville: Bibliographical Society of the University of Virginia, 1954. 200 p.

Prefatory material and captions are in English and German. Contains 2,989 items arranged by subject field; provides a name and subject index.

STILLWELL, MARGARET B.
Incunábula in American Libraries: A Second Census of Fifteenth Century Books owned in the United States, Mexico, and Canada. New York: Bibliographical Society of America, 1940. 619 p.

In the Census of Fifteenth Century Books Owned in America published in 1919, the Preface notes that "an estimate of 13,200 copies is recorded under 6,292 titles, owned by 173 public and 255 private collections." The second census lists

"35,232 copies of 11,132 titles, owned by 232 public and 390 private collections. And of these 35,232 copies, 28,491 copies are owned by institutions, and 6,741 copies are in private hands."

Each entry includes author's name, Hain numbers, short title, place, printer, date, catalogs, and location.

TUCKER, LENA AND ALLEN BENHAM.
A Bibliography of Fifteenth Century Literature: With Special Reference to the History of English Culture. Seattle, Washington: University of Washington Press, 1928. 274 p.

Aims to bring together in usable form the material which would be available in a university or research library. Makes no attempt to list manuscripts, first or rare editions. References to these are found in the general bibliography section, as well as in the individual author bibliographies. The main divisions are: Bibliography; Political Background; Social and Economic Background; Cultural Background; Linguistic Background; Literature; Appendix.

The work, "in spite of its title is a bibliography, not of the original texts, but of modern works concerning the 15th century literature. A large number of titles are listed, among them many articles in periodicals which were well worth recording. Unfortunately, the system of classification is unscientific and will not give the reader much assistance in finding what he wants"—(YEAR'S WORK IN ENGLISH STUDIES, XXVII).

"It is to be regretted that this volume, containing much valuable reference material, should have issued from the press without the benefit of those labors of analysis and revision which would have made it a work of less limited usefulness"—(MODERN LANGUAGE NOTES, VOLUME 46).

WELLS, JOHN E.
Manual of the Writings in Middle English 1050–1400. Published under the Auspices of the Connecticut Academy of Arts and Sciences. 1941. 941 p.

Attempts to treat all the extant writings in print, "from single lines to the most extensive pieces, composed in English between 1050 and 1400." For each piece included, provides probable date, MS or MSS, form and extent, dialect in which first composed, source or sources, bibliography, comment, and, in some cases, abstracts.

The index covers every reference to each work; cross references are numerous. The main work covers bibliography to September, 1915. The first eight supplements include additions and modifications to December, 1941. The ninth supplement, July, 1951, includes additions and modifications to December, 1945.

"A long step towards the writing of the history of medieval literature in England will have been accomplished when the work of such manuals as this of Professor Wells, which engages our notice shall have been fully understood by the critical world. . . . The wideness and fulness of the author's own reading, the evidence on every page that no work has escaped an individual and independent judgment by the compiler, render the work peculiarly valuable to those who have no time for the original. For such the book is more than a bibliographic manual; it is distinctly informative in an encyclopedia way"—(YALE REVIEW, VOL. VI, 659–660).

"The work is well-done and serves at least two purposes, in that it affords a complete view for the first time of a large body of literature, and provides the fullest possible information short of a critical edition, of any given piece to which reference may be sought. It is particularly useful for indicating where the text of such and such a piece may be found"—(LONDON TIMES LITERARY SUPPLEMENT, September 14, 443).

WELLS, JOHN EDWIN.

Ninth Supplement to A Manual of the Writings in Middle English, 1050–1400. New Haven, Conn.: Yale University Press, 1951. pp. 1779–1938.

Additions to and modifications of the basic volume and supplements to December, 1945, by Beatrice Daw Brown, Eleanor K. Heningham, and Francis Lee Utley.

CURRENT

Annual Bibliography of English Language and Literature, 1920—. Edited for the Modern Humanities Research Association. London: Cambridge University Press, 1921–. Annual. (Volume 20, covering the year 1939, was published in 1948; volume 21, covering the year 1940, was published in 1950; volume 22, covering the year 1941, was published in 1952; and volume 23, covering the year 1942, was published in 1952.

An excellent annual bibliography of English and American literature; aims to provide as complete a list as possible of all the books and articles of value which deal with the English language and literature appearing in the previous year. Includes references to all important reviews in British, American, and foreign periodicals, and thus enables the student to obtain varied and authoritative comment on most works of significance. Publication was suspended during the war, but an attempt is now being made to bring the work up to date.

"A fairly prolonged check has revealed only three minor misprints—a sufficient testimony to the quality of the work of both editor and printers. The volume maintains the reputation of the series as an invaluable aid to scholarship"—(MODERN LANGUAGE REVIEW, XLIII, 561).

Progress of Medieval and Renaissance Studies in the United States and Canada: Colorado: University of Colorado Press, 1923–.

The first number was limited to historical studies and contained the names of sixty medievalists. The second number was expanded to include those interested in medieval Latin studies. The third number, appearing in 1925, and representing a distinct departure from earlier issues, sought to embrace all phases of interest in the medieval period. The fifteenth number marked the addition of renaissance studies.

Each issue includes: a section entitled General Matters—papers read at learned societies, for example; lists of works published (including publication facts) and a notation as to their being or not being doctoral dissertations, and a list of doctoral dissertations in progress.

Research in Progress in the Modern Languages and Literatures, 1948–. (In PMLA, Vol. 63, Supplement, pt. 2, pp. 143–405.)

Takes up the function of WORK IN PROGRESS, previously published by the MODERN HUMANITIES RESEARCH ASSOCIATION, suspended in 1942. Lists research in progress in twenty-nine countries. Contains a subject and author index. The latter also serves as an index to the addresses of 3,550 scholars in various countries.

Speculum: A Journal of Medieval Studies. Cambridge, Massachusetts: The Medieval Academy of America, 1926–.

Each issue of this quarterly journal contains a bibliography of the periodical literature in the Medieval period that appeared during the preceding quarter. Often publishes articles intended to illuminate neglected areas and to open up new fields of research. Publishes reviews.

"MODERN LANGUAGE NOTES extends greetings to SPECULUM, a new mirror through which students of the modern languages may become more richly conscious of their medieval heritage. . . . Of the significance for research in the humanities which this movement connotes there is no need to speak. The officers of the academy and the editors of the journal are men who have won distinction in the classics, in history, in architecture, and in modern scholarship. . . . Since art, beauty and poetry are portions of our medieval heritage, all will be presented in studies that are scholarly and arranged in pleasing form. The journal will also combine detail with synthesis"—(MODERN LANGUAGE NOTES, XLI).

Work in Progress . . . in the Modern Humanities, 1938–1942. Cambridge: Modern Humanities Research Association, 1938–1942.

The predecessor of RESEARCH IN PROGRESS (see pages 139–140). No longer published.

Year's Work in English Studies. Edited for the English Association. London: Oxford University Press, 1921–.

The ANNUAL BIBLIOGRAPHY OF ENGLISH LANGUAGE AND LITERATURE includes American literature. The YEAR'S WORK IN ENGLISH STUDIES excludes American literature, but embraces comparable areas of English literature as the former, listing fewer titles, but giving brief comment. Emphasis of treatment varies with the occasion. Thus the 1924 issue gives special attention to philology and, since the year represented the Byron centenary, also to the Romantic Movement; whereas the 1928 issue, the year marking the tercentenary of Bunyan's death, provides particular consideration of the Restoration. The later editions of the YEAR'S WORK follow the same pattern and policy of the earlier volumes; the main difference resides in the matter of items listed.

"Each period of literature is supervised by a specialist, who combines summary and assessment very skillfully without arrogance or leniency"—(LONDON TIMES LITERARY SUPPLEMENT, February 15, 1923, 104).

"This volume [XXXV] maintains a steady standard of fullness and judiciousness. The design of the book has been tightened up, with fuller page and smaller, yet quite legible type, all of which keeps it within manageable size, without reducing scope of survey, which continues to astonish by its completeness"—(MODERN LANGUAGE REVIEW, 1954).

Year's Work in Modern Language Studies. Edited for the MODERN HUMANITIES RESEARCH ASSOCIATION. Cambridge: University Press, 1951. Vols. 1–10, 1931–1940; Vol. XI, 1940–1949; Vol. XII, 1950.

The work is edited by a number of scholars; covers medieval Latin, Italian, French, Hispanic, Roumanian, Germanic, and Celtic studies, and, in later volumes, International languages and slavonic studies.

DISSERTATIONS

Dissertation Abstracts: A Guide to Dissertations and Monographs Available in Microform. Ann Arbor, Michigan: University Microfilms, 1952—.

Formerly called MICROFILM ABSTRACTS. The change in title and format begins with Volume 12, No. 1, 1952. Six issues are published each year, one containing author and subject indexes for the year. Now only available on a subscription basis.

Doctoral Dissertations Accepted by American Universities. Compiled for the Association of Research Libraries. New York: Wilson, 1934–. Annual.

Twenty-two volumes appeared between the years 1933–1950. The general division of each volume falls typically into seven categories: philosophy, religion, physical sciences, social sciences, and humanities. The arrangement within the various subdivisions is alphabetical by university and by author. The main contents are: Alphabetical Subject Index; Publication and Preservation of American Doctoral Dissertations; List of Periodic University Publications Abstracting Dissertations; Statistical Tables; Lists of Dissertations arranged by Subject.

The entries include the name of the author, the title of his work, and, if the thesis is published, a bibliographical description of it. Also contains a tabular listing of the distribution of doctorates by school and subject, and an author index.

"This volume provides a very useful and complete list of doctoral dissertations accepted during the past year. . . . Much valuable information is given in the introductory pages. A 'Table of Practice of Publication and Loan of Doctoral Dissertations' gives in convenient form information which has been found heretofore only through the trial-and-error method"—(THE LIBRARY QUARTERLY, April, 1935, 250).

Indexes to Theses Accepted for Higher Degrees in the Universities of Great Britain and Ireland. Edited by P. D. Record. London: ASLIB, 1953–.

An annual classified list, alphabetically arranged by university under various heads. Information includes author's name, title of thesis, and degree granted. Contains both subject and author indexes.

List of American Doctoral Dissertations Printed in 1912–1928. Washington, D.C.: Government Printing Office, 1913–1940. 26 vols.

Each volume has four divisions: (1) an alphabetical list of titles; (2) a subject list, classified by the Library of Congress indexing system; (3) a subject index; (4) a list of authors, arranged according to the institutions granting the degrees. Includes some forty-five colleges and universities. No longer published.

Microfilm Abstracts: A Collection of Abstracts of Doctoral Dissertations and Monographs Which Are Available in Complete Form on Microfilm. Ann Arbor, Michigan: University Microfilms, 1938– .

This collection of abstracts is distributed to leading libraries and journals accompanied by printed library cards for each abstract. The dissertations themselves are microfilmed in full and copies of the microfilm are available for sale through University Microfilm. Now called DISSERTATION ABSTRACTS.

PALFREY, T. H., H. E. COLEMAN, JR.
Guide to Bibliographies of Theses, United States and Canada. 2d ed. Chicago: American Library Association, 1940. 54 p.

Nothing appears to be known about the first edition. The second edition comprises general lists, lists in special fields, and institutional lists. The third edition was printed in 1950. The arrangement is alphabetical throughout–in the third grouping, according to the schools listed.

"This is a helpful tool for college and university libraries. It contains a reasonably complete listing of theses [although] a few omissions are noted"–(WILSON LIBRARY BULLETIN, 15:683).

"This guide furnishes a convenient aid for the student wishing to know what research work has been completed in his field. For the library itself it is most useful in locating reference materials"–(LIBRARY QUARTERLY, 7:287).

Progress of Medieval and Renaissance Studies in the United States and Canada. (See annotation on page 139.)

ROSENBERG, RALPH P.
Bibliographies of Theses in America. (In the BULLETIN OF BIBLIOGRAPHY for September–December, 1945, and January–April, 1946.)

Constitutes a supplement to GUIDE TO BIBLIOGRAPHIES (Palfrey and Coleman), with corrections and additions.

RENAISSANCE AND RESTORATION

GENERAL

HAZLITT, WILLIAM CAREW.
Handbook to the Popular, Poetical, and Dramatic Literature of Great Britain, From the Invention of Printing to the Restoration. London: J. R. Smith, 1867. 701 p.

A two-column format, alphabetically arranged according to author. Bibliographical Collections and Notes on Early English Literature, 1474–1700 (London: Quaritch, 1876–1903) in six volumes, a useful supplement, is alphabetically arranged according to title. Also serviceable is G. J. Gray's GENERAL INDEX TO HAZLITT'S HANDBOOK AND HIS BIBLIOGRAPHICAL COLLECTIONS (London: Quaritch, 1893, 866 p.), which indexes the HANDBOOK and all the volumes of the Bibliographical Collections except the fourth series and the second supplement to the third series.

POLLARD, ALFRED W. and G. R. REDGRAVE.
Short-Title Catalogue of Books Printed in England, Scotland, and Ireland, and of English Books Printed Abroad, 1475–1640. London: Bibliographical Society, 1926. 609 p.

A comprehensive record of English books (some 26,000) arranged according to author. Contains abridged entries of all the English books, copies of which exist at the British Museum, the Bodleian, the Cambridge University Library, and the Henry E. Huntington Library, California. For each entry gives: author, brief title, size, printer, date, reference to entry of the book in the Stationers' registers, and location. Of the libraries referred to, 133 are British, 15 are American. It is supplemented by the Huntington Library Supplement compiled by C. K. Edmonds and published by the Harvard University Press in 1933.

"This catalog lists 26,143 books and locates for us two copies in Great Britain and two copies in America wherever possible; and in cases where a book is very rare tries to locate all of the known copies. . . . By means of correspondence, copies of a vast number of books can be located for scholars in this country, but in this SHORT TITLE CATALOG with each of its items serially numbered, we have an opportunity, at a relatively small cost in editorial work and printing, to place in the hands of our librarians and scholars a finding list of inestimable value"—(LIBRARY JOURNAL, 52:816).

TANNENBAUM, S. and D. R. TANNENBAUM.
Elizabethan Bibliographies. New York: The Author, 1937–1947. No. 1–39.

Brief bibliographies of primary and secondary works, including bibliographies of the sonnets and five plays of Shakespeare (MACBETH, KING LEAR, MERCHANT OF VENICE, OTHELLO, TROILUS AND CRESSIDA). Some of the bibliographies are quite short (Cyril Tourner, 14 p.). Others are relatively long (MACBETH, 165 p., BEN JONSON, 151 p., THE MERCHANT OF VENICE, 140 p.).

WING, DONALD GODDARD.
Short-Title Catalogue of Books Printed in England, Scotland, Ireland, Wales, and British America and of English Books Printed in Other Countries, 1641–1700. New York: Columbia University Press, 1948–1951. 3 v.

A continuation of Pollard and Redgrave, SHORT-TITLE CATALOGUE. Locates items in more than 200 libraries, many items being given five locations in Great Britain and five locations in America. Location symbols, however, are in accordance with a system devised by the author, not in accordance with the system followed by the S.T.C. or the UNION CATALOG.

"It was a daring, hazardous and some would say foolhardy undertaking for one man, and if the achievement falls a long way short of perfection, this is not to say that Mr. Wing has not made a most important and serviceable contribution to enumerative bibliography"—(LONDON TIMES LITERARY SUPPLEMENT, November 14, 1952).

CURRENT

Annual Bibliography of English Language and Literature, 1920–. Edited for the MODERN HUMANITIES RESEARCH ASSOCIATION. London: Cambridge University Press, 1921–. (For annotation, see pages 139–140.)

Philological Quarterly: A Journal Devoted to Scholarly Investigation in the Classical and Modern Languages and Literatures. Iowa City: State University of Iowa Press, 1922–. (For annotation see pages 97–98.)

Progress of Medieval and Renaissance Studies in the United States and Canada. Colorado: University of Colorado Press, 1923–. (For annotation see page 139.)

Research in Progress in the Modern Languages and Literatures, 1948–. (In PMLA, Vol. 63, Supplement, pt. 2, pp. 143–405.) (For annotation, see pages 139–140.)

Studies in Philology. Chapel Hill, North Carolina: University of North Carolina Press, 1906–. (For annotation see page 100.)

Work in Progress . . . in the Modern Humanities, 1938–1942. Cambridge: MODERN HUMANITIES RESEARCH ASSOCIATION, 1938–1942.

The predecessor of RESEARCH IN PROGRESS. No longer published.

Year's Work in English Studies. Edited for the English Association. London: Oxford University Press, 1921–. (For annotation see pages 140–141.)

DISSERTATIONS

For an annotated list of dissertations which are useful to the student of the Renaissance and Restoration periods, see pages 141–143.

EIGHTEENTH CENTURY

GENERAL

CRANE, RONALD S., LOUIS I. BREDVOLD.
English Literature, 1660–1800: A Bibliography of Modern Studies. Compiled for PHILOLOGICAL QUARTERLY. Princeton:

Princeton University Press, 1950–1952. Vol. I, 575 p., Vol. II, 579–1292.

Volume I includes reprints of the annual bibliographies published in the PHILOLOGICAL QUARTERLY 1926–1938, covering studies published 1925–1937; Volume II includes reprints of the annual bibliographies published in the PHILOLOGICAL QUARTERLY 1939–1950, covering studies published 1938–1949, and an index to both volumes. In a single alphabet, the index lists: (1) the names of modern scholars whose books and articles have been listed; (2) the names of those who have been the subjects of the studies; (3) topical entries—names of periodicals, place names, themes; (4) selected miscellaneous entries—e.g., Gothic voyages. The basic classifications, within which works are arranged in a chronological order according to authors' surnames, are: (1) Bibliography and Bibliographical Studies; (2) Language; (3) Historical and Social Background; (4) Philosophy, Science, and Religion; (5) Arts and Crafts; (6) Literary History and Criticism; (7) Individual Authors; (8) Continental Background. The reviews of books listed are often very full, scholarly, and readable.

"The annotations are generally impressive. The lists of abbreviations show that the search of the periodicals has been thorough. In particular attention has been paid to NOTES AND QUERIES, a journal which is far too often overlooked. . . . A full study of the present volume shows that the book is indispensable to members of English faculties, and can be usefully consulted by readers of literature generally"—(LONDON TIMES LITERARY SUPPLEMENT, September 28, 1952).

TOBIN, JAMES E.
Eighteenth Century English Literature and Its Cultural Background. New York: Fordham University Press, 1939. 190 p.

Contains over 7,000 titles, exclusive of diaries, autobiographies, and journals, representing primary and secondary works. Part I includes: (1) Historical Background; (2) Social Thought; (3) Memoirs, Diaries, Anecdotes; (4) Criticism; (5) Poetry; (6) Prose; (7) Journalism; (8) Drama; (9) Extra National Relations. Part II contains the bibliographies of 169 individual authors (pp. 67–180). Does not provide annotations.

"Professor Tobin has performed a meritorious service by

collecting within the covers of one volume a selection of this voluminous material and making it available in convenient form. . . . Brief critical notes appended to some of the titles would have increased the bulk of the volume, but would have immeasurably heightened its value. . . . American journals have been combed more thoroughly than foreign; the files of the Athenaeum, particularly, would have yielded a number of important items"—(LIBRARY QUARTERLY, July, 1940, 446–448).

CURRENT

Annual Bibliography of English Language and Literature, 1920—. Edited for the MODERN HUMANITIES RESEARCH ASSOCIATION. London: Cambridge University Press, 1921—. Annual. (For annotation see pages 138–139.)

Philological Quarterly: A Journal Devoted to Scholarly Investigation in the Classical and Modern Languages and Literatures. Iowa City: State University of Iowa Press, 1922—. (For annotation see pages 97–98.)

Research in Progress in the Modern Languages and Literature, 1948—. (In PMLA, Vol. 63, Supplement, pt. 2, pp. 143–405). (For annotation see pages 139–140.)

Work in Progress . . . in the Modern Humanities, 1938–1942. Cambridge: MODERN HUMANITIES RESEARCH ASSOCIATION, 1938–1942. (For annotation see page 140.)

Year's Work in English Studies. Edited for the English Association. London: Oxford University Press, 1921—. (For annotation see pages 140–141.)

DISSERTATIONS

For an annotated list of dissertations which are useful to the student of the Eighteenth Century, see pages 141–143.

NINETEENTH CENTURY

GENERAL

DERBY, J. RAYMOND, ED.
The Romantic Movement: A Selective and Critical Bibliography. In PHILOLOGICAL QUARTERLY, Vol. 29, 1950–.

Continues the bibliography edited by Walter Graham [and others] and previously published in ELH.

EHRSAM, THEODORE G., ROBERT DEILY.
BIBLIOGRAPHIES OF TWELVE VICTORIAN AUTHORS. New York: H. W. Wilson, 1936. 362 p.

The authors treated are: Elizabeth Barrett Browning, Matthew Arnold, Arthur Clough, Edward Fitzgerald, Thomas Hardy, Rudyard Kipling, William Morris, Christina Rossetti, Robert Louis Stevenson, Charles Swinburne, and Alfred Lord Tennyson. The matter is compiled from over two hundred sources and is divided into biographies, pamphlets, bibliographies, essays, critical analysis, foreign material, unpublished articles, doctoral dissertations, and unpublished master's theses.

"The compilers have done a valuable and lasting piece of work which will inevitably place students of Victorian poetry heavily in their debt"–(MODERN PHILOLOGY, 1936–1937).

"An immense amount of work has gone into the preparation of the bibliographies in this volume. . . . it is distinctly a scholarly book"–(LIBRARY QUARTERLY, 1937, 161–162).

FAVERTY, FREDERIC EVERETT.
The Victorian Poets: A Guide to Research. Cambridge, Mass.: Harvard University Press, 1956. 292 p.

A handbook of "bibliography, scholarship, and criticism. Chapters by specialists are devoted to major authors separately, to minor authors and movements collectively.

RAYSOR, THOMAS M.
English Romantic Poets: A Review of Research. New York: Modern Language Association of America, 1950. 395 p.

Aims to assist the graduate student as he begins his specialized study of the field of English Romanticism. Includes Wordsworth, Coleridge, Byron, Shelley, and Keats. Lists studies of ideas, general and miscellaneous criticism, and additional references on individual poems. Major works are discussed at relative length; minor works are characterized in a sentence or two. Has no index.

". . . a godsend to graduate students and almost equally, to practising specialists in the fields of English Romantic poetry. . . . The absence of an index is by all means the most serious defect of the book. It is inexplicable and deplorable that a book produced under the auspices of an association dedicated to preserving and propagating the highest standards of scholarly publication should lack a feature no scholarly volume—least of all, a collection of bibliographical essays—should be without"—(PHILOLOGICAL QUARTERLY, XXX, April, 1951, 100–101).

"In ENGLISH ROMANTIC Poets, six of the best American Scholars have united to produce a book whose modest title is misleading . . . have, in fact, provided not only the graduate beginning research, but more advanced students with a succession of bibliographies, and, in addition, wise and balanced and sometimes witty comments"—(MODERN LANGUAGE REVIEW, XLVI, 547).

RAYSOR, THOMAS MIDDLETON.
The English Romantic Poets: A Review of Research. Rev. ed. New York: Modern Language Association of America, 1956. 307 p.

This, a revised edition of the work published in 1950, constitutes a companion volume to the Faverty title.

TEMPLEMAN, WILLIAM D.
Bibliographies of Studies in Victorian Literature for the Thirteen Years 1932–1944. Urbana: University of Illinois Press, 1945. 450 p.

A photoprint of bibliographies published originally in the May issues of MODERN PHILOLOGY, 1933–1945. The main divisions are: (1) Individual Authors; (2) Material Contributed from the Continent; (3) Bibliographical Material; (4) Movements of

Ideas and Literary Forms; (5) Anthologies. The additions to the original issues of MODERN PHILOLOGY are simply: a preface, a foreword by Howard Mumford Jones, and a helpful index.

"But his attempt is insufficient; mere aggregation is not cumulation, and a scholar who pays five dollars for the volume might fairly expect it to be something more than the thirteen parts he already had in his file of MODERN PHILOLOGY. The brief index of names that has been added tells us only that items are listed each year under major authors, and somewhat intermittently for those who attract less interest; the skeleton given is not a living index. . . . Because of the photographic reproduction all the page references to earlier numbers of the annual bibliography are wrong—a considerable nuisance. The volume is on the whole a convenience, but it contributes little to the solution of the scholar's problem"—(LIBRARY QUARTERLY, 1945–1946, 362–364).

TOWNSEND, FRANCIS G., ED.
Victorian Bibliography, 1957—. In VICTORIAN STUDIES, Vol. 1, June 1958—.

Continues the list previously published in MODERN PHILOLOGY.

WRIGHT, AUSTIN.
Bibliographies of Studies in Victorian Literature, 1945–1954. Urbana: University of Illinois Press, 1956.

Supplements Templeman's BIBLIOGRAPHIES OF STUDIES IN VICTORIAN LITERATURE FOR THE THIRTEEN YEARS 1932–1944. Each chapter (an annual) contains a brief introduction, general information, and a key of abbreviations. The major divisions of each annual are arranged alphabetically under four headings: (I) Bibliographical Material; (II) Economic, Political, Religious, and Social Environment; (III) Movements of Ideas and Literary Forms; (IV) Individual Authors. The Index comprises a single alphabetical arrangement of the names of authors listed, of Victorian figures written about or mentioned, of selected place names, and of headings relating to background.

"A valuable guide to the work done in the study of Victorian literature, both here and in America, during the ten years, and with editorial notes to indicate the content and importance of the items listed"—(LONDON TIMES LITERARY SUPPLEMENT, Oct. 5, 1956, 591).

"The Index is greatly superior to that of 1945. Cross references are useful. A comprehensive "Key to Abbreviations" among the preliminary matter would be an asset. Wright and his ten compilers should be congratulated for their industry and ability. This text will be of great value to students of the period and to all reference librarians"—(LIBRARY JOURNAL, VOL. 82, 2342).

CURRENT

Annual Bibliography of English Language and Literature, 1920—. For the publication facts and description of contents, see pages 139–140.

English Literary History; A Journal of English Literary History. For the publication facts and a description of the basic contents see page 92.

Modern Philology. For the publication facts and a description of contents, see page 97.

Philological Quarterly. For the publication facts and a description of contents, see pages 97–98.

Research in Progress in the Modern Languages and Literature, 1948—. For the publication facts and a description of contents, see pages 139–140.

Work in Progress. For the publication facts and a description of contents, see page 140.

Year's Work in English Studies. For the publication facts and a description of contents, see pages 254–255.

DISSERTATIONS

For an annotated list of dissertations useful to the student of the nineteenth century consult pages 141–143.

TWENTIETH CENTURY

GENERAL

MILLETT, FRED B.

Contemporary British Literature: A Critical Survey and 232 Author Bibliographies. Third revised and enlarged edition, based upon the second revised and enlarged edition by J. M. Manly and Edith Rickert. New York: Harcourt, 1935. 556 p.

Something more than a revision and expansion. Contains a 110 page "Critical Survey," discussing general background, the bibliographies of some forty authors not included in the earlier edition, and excludes some thirty authors treated in the earlier edition. The arrangement is alphabetical by writer. Provides a short biography for each author, a fairly complete bibliography of his works (with date of publication only), and biographical and critical studies or reviews arranged alphabetically by author or magazine.

"In general . . . this book has been thoroughly edited and presents a great mass of material in a very convenient form. Librarians, scholars, and students can all make use of this handy reference work"—(LIBRARY JOURNAL, LXI, 108).

"The bibliographies themselves are remarkably full for a work of this kind, and endeavor to list the first appearance, in the British Empire or elsewhere, of every book and pamphlet by the author in question published before January 1, 1935, including translations, but excluding "edited works," such as anthologies. This limitation is rather regrettable, and rules out important books such as Mrs. Meynell's FLOWER OF THE MIND, and Mr. de la Mare's COME HITHER. Pseudonyms are unveiled, and sometimes with surprising results"—(LONDON TIMES LITERARY SUPPLEMENT, January 4, 1936, 17).

CURRENT

Annual Bibliography of English Language and Literature, 1920—. For the publication facts and description of contents, see pages 138–139.

Research in Progress in the Modern Languages and Literature, 1948—. For the publication facts and a description of contents, see pages 139–140.

Work in Progress. For the publication facts and a description of contents, see page 140.

DISSERTATIONS

For an annotated list of dissertations useful to the student of the twentieth century consult pages 141–143.

AMERICAN LITERATURE

GENERAL

BLANCK, Joseph.
Bibliography of American Literature. New Haven: Yale University Press, 1955—. Vol. 1—.

This is the first volume of a projected eight or nine volume work, sponsored by the Bibliographical Society of America, which, when completed, will include the works published in book form of some three hundred writers from the beginning of the Federal period up to and including persons who died before the end of 1930. Volume I covers Henry Adams to Donn Byrne, 3,200 entries of forty-one authors. Under each author, the material, listed chronologically, includes: (1) first editions of books and pamphlets (including full title, publication facts, collation, and other bibliographical details); (2) reprints containing textual or other changes; (3) A selected list of biographical, bibliographical, and critical works. Location is given for copies examined.

"Volume I has been carefully done, and gives promise that Mr. Blanck and his associates and sponsors will make a monumental contribution, not only to bibliography, but also to the study of American Literature"—(U.S. QUARTERLY BOOK REVIEW, VOL. 12).

"The study is so thorough that this seems to be the definitive work on its subject. . . . Here is a great encyclopedia of bibliography with which every student of American literature will be delighted and by which he will be aided"—(AMERICAN LITERATURE, VOLUME 28).

"This BIBLIOGRAPHY OF AMERICAN LITERATURE is "skeletal, monumental, and authoritative. It replaces Merle Johnson as he replaced Foley. It holds its place with Allibone, the CAMBRIDGE HISTORY OF AMERICAN LITERATURE, and the post World War II bibliography of Spiller. Collectors will consider it essential and textual students will discover it to be 'exasperatingly helpful' "—(THE BOOK COLLECTOR, SUMMER, 1956, 185–186).

BLANCK, JOSEPH.
Bibliography of American Literature. New Haven: Yale University Press, 1957—.

The second volume of a projected eight or nine volume work.

CANTRELL, CLYDE H. AND PATRICK, WALTON R.
Southern Literary Culture: A Bibliography of Masters' and Doctors' Theses. Tuscaloosa: University of Alabama, 1955. 124 p.

A list of masters' and doctors' theses completed through the summer of 1948 in the graduate schools of the United States, dealing with southern culture and literature.

EVANS, CHARLES.
American Bibliography: A Chronological Dictionary of all Books, Pamphlets, and Periodical Publications Printed in the United States of America from the Genesis of Printing in 1639 Down to and Including the Year 1820; with Bibliographical and Biographical Notes. Chicago: Columbia Press, 1903–1934. Vols. 1–12.

For further comment see page 232.

FOLEY, PATRICK K.
American Authors, 1795–1895. A Bibliography of First and Notable Editions Chronologically Arranged with Notes. With an Introduction by W. L. Sawyer. Boston: Publishers' Printing Company, 1897. 350 p.

When published in 1897, it was the most useful work of its kind; although now out-of-date, it still retains some value: It provides:

(1) an indication of authors and works that were considered notable at the time; (2) it may serve as a supplement to the CHAL and, when completed, to Blanck's BIBLIOGRAPHY OF AMERICAN LITERATURE for the period 1795–1895.

"Of the 300 authors given, over thirty are unknown even by name to the reviewer, who has been acquainted with the writings of his own countrymen for many years. The omissions are most glaring, among them being Charles A. Dana, Emily Dickinson, Horace Greely, Judge O. W. Holmes, Henry James, and Herbert D. Ward. . . . It is a fairly accurate checklist of the American authors it includes. It contains, also, much information generally unknown before, and is a step in advance of 'Leon's' and 'Stone's' but it falls far short of its opportunities" —(THE CRITIC, September 4, 1897, 123–124).

FULLERTON, BRADFORD M.
A Selective Bibliography of American Literature, 1775–1900. New York: William Payson, 1932.

The aim of the book is to briefly estimate the more important American authors, and to describe their more representative works. The authors are listed alphabetically. Has no index.

"Bradford M. Fullerton manifests fine selective judgement, not merely in the authors presented, but in the details related of them; included are all the writers whom we would expect to find, and many of the less prominent whom we are surprised and also pleased to see. Accuracy and brevity are combined with an interest that only first-hand familiarity with his matter could give"—(AMERICA, XLVIII, 487).

"Mr. Fullerton's SELECTIVE BIBLIOGRAPHY is a handbook that both dispenser and absorber of American first editions must whole-heartedly welcome. If it did nothing but chart new or little trod paths it would fulfill an eminently praiseworthy purpose, but it does more than that. For Mr. Fullerton has made of what might easily have been as arid a performance as a telephone directory a readable as well as a serviceable manual" —(THE SATURDAY REVIEW OF LITERATURE, X, 321).

LEARY, LEWIS GASTON.
Articles on American Literature, 1900–1950. Durham, North Carolina: Duke University Press, 1954. 437 p.

A revision and extension of ARTICLES ON AMERICAN LITERATURE, APPEARING IN CURRENT PERIODICALS, 1920–1945. The main part of the work comprises an alphabetical list of articles about the American authors (the American authors being the basis of the arrangement), followed by subject and form groupings.

MILLETT, FRED B.
Contemporary American Authors: A Critical Survey and 219 Bio-bibliographies. New York: Harcourt, 1940. 716 p.

A revised and expanded edition of the work of Manly and Rickert. Contains a lengthy critical survey of American literature since 1900 (pp. 1–204). The main part of the text comprises biographical and bibliographical information and a list of studies and articles about the author. The foreword notes: "107 authors have been dropped from the second edition; six authors who were dropped in the second edition have been restored; 30 authors who appeared for the first time in the second edition have been retained and 101 new authors have been added.

"For it is certainly the finest large scale bibliography of contemporary American literature to be issued within the covers of one volume. . . . The book unquestionably belongs in every library and on the desk of every student of contemporary literature"—(THE CHRISTIAN CENTURY, March 6, 1940, 321).

". . . a variety of checkings have led me to a respectful confidence in the accuracy of the book. And I have not only examined it: I am referring to it all the time" (a review of the original edition by P. H. Boynton, NEW REPUBLIC, January 3, 1923).

RUSK, RALPH L.
The Literature of the Middle Western Frontier. New York: Columbia University Press, 1925. 2 vols.

A comprehensive survey and bibliography of the literature of the West before 1840. Volume one contains a history of the pioneer period and a discussion of such interests as cultural beginnings, newspapers and magazines, controversial writings, and fiction. Volume two is a bibliographical volume, following the arrangement of the companion volume, and covering: cultural beginnings, travel, newspapers, and magazines, controversial writings, scholarly writings, and schoolbooks, fiction, poetry, and drama. Locates copies.

"With the utmost thoroughness and impartiality, Dr. Rusk has traversed every department of literature within his period. . . . His painstaking bibliography will be of permanent value to students of early American literature"—(NORTH AMERICAN REVIEW, CCXII, 1925, 354–357).

"This is a laborious, learned, and useful contribution to the history of the West. It represents a relatively clean sweep of the material on the literary aspect of Western culture, classifying with intelligence and appraising with fairness. . . . We need more books like this, dealing with the bed-rock of Western fact"—(AMERICAN HISTORICAL REVIEW, VOLUME 31, 366).

SABIN, JOSEPH.
Dictionary of Books Relating to America from Its Discovery to the Present Time. New York: Bibliographical Society of America, 1928–1936. 29 v.

For an annotation consult pages 128–129.

SPILLER, ROBERT E. [AND OTHERS].
Literary History of the United States. New York: Macmillan, 1948. 3 vols.

Volume I constitutes a history of American literature from Colonial beginnings to the Civil War; Volume II constitutes a history of American literature from the end of the Civil War to the present; Volume III constitutes the Bibliography, the main divisions of which are: Guide to resources; Literature and culture; Movements and Influences; and Individual authors. In addition to the 207 individual author bibliographies there is information on separate and collected works, edited texts and reprints, biography and criticism, primary sources, and bibliographies. Volumes one and two have no footnotes; volume three contains an author and subject index.

"Editors and contributors seem to have no clear conception of their function as either literary historians or literary critics. They are little concerned with theories as to how a literary history should be written. They have a great concern with social backgrounds and implications of our literature. The soundest discussions are those which sum up what is known and thought about the major writers in New England. The weakest chapters are those about writers and topics which have attracted little attention from scholars. The least satisfactory chapters are on twentieth century authors and on writers of the South and West in all periods"—(SOUTH ATLANTIC QUARTERLY, 48:452–467).

TRENT, WILLIAM P. [AND OTHERS].
Cambridge History of American Literature. New York: Putnam, 1917–1921. 4 vols.

The 1954 reissue by Macmillan in three volumes is textually complete, but lacks the bibliographies (indexed in Northup's REGISTER) which are an important feature of the original edition.

Volume one covers colonial and revolutionary literature; volume two, early and later national literature; volumes three and four, later national literature. In its time, and perhaps at present, the most important history of American literature.

"A valuable, comprehensive, and from beginning to end, a more interesting book. Emphasis must be laid upon the care and detail which the authors and editors have devoted to the early literature of our land . . . is of the utmost importance"—(THE NEW YORK TIMES, November 25, 1917).

"This history brings to our notice writers whom we should otherwise have overlooked; fills up gaps in our knowledge of the literary history of the country, and supplies accurate data as to the various activities of the press and the biographies of writers"—(SATURDAY REVIEW OF LITERATURE, May 31, 1919).

"This lack of balance, together with the lack of contagious enthusiasm in the writing, and the dearth of comparative estimates, constitute in our view faults which prevent us from extending such a cordial reception to the second volume as we did to the first"—(THE TIMES LITERARY SUPPLEMENT, July 17, 1919).

CURRENT

American Literature, 1929–. North Carolina: Duke University Press, 1929–. For an annotation see pages 91–92.

Annual Bibliography of English Language and Literature, 1920–. Edited for the MODERN HUMANITIES RESEARCH ASSOCIATION. See pages 138–139.

Publications of the Modern Language Association of America. Baltimore, 1884–.

For an annotation see pages 98–99.

DISSERTATIONS

Dissertation Abstracts: A Guide to Dissertations and Monographs Available in Microform. Ann Arbor, Michigan: University Microfilms, 1952–. (For an annotation see page 141.)

Doctoral Dissertations Accepted by American Universities. Compiled for the Association of Research Libraries. New York: Wilson, 1934–. Annual. (For an annotation, consult page 142.)

LEARY, LEWIS G.
Doctoral Dissertations in American Literature, 1933–1948. Durham, North Carolina: Duke University Press, 1950. 230 p.

Basically a reprint from the May, 1948 issue of AMERICAN LITERATURE, with corrections and additional titles. Dissertations in progress are printed in roman type; those completed are printed in italics. Titles are listed alphabetically in two groups: (1) "Dissertations on Individual Authors"; (2) "Dissertations on General Topics."

LEISY, ERNEST E. AND JAY B. HUBBELL.
Doctoral Dissertations in American Literature. Durham, North Carolina: Duke University Press, 1933.

Basically a reprint from the May, 1933 issue of AMERICAN LITERATURE, with corrections and some additional titles.

List of American Doctoral Dissertations Printed in 1912–1928. Washington, D.C.: Government Printing Office, 1913–1940. 26 vols. (For an annotation see pages 142–143.)

Microfilm Abstracts: A Collection of Abstracts of Doctoral Dissertations and Monographs Which are Available in Complete Form on Microfilm. Ann Arbor, Michigan: University Microfilms, 1938–. (For an annotation see page 143.)

PALFREY, T. H., H. E. COLEMAN.
Guide to Bibliographies of Theses, United States and Canada. 2d ed. Chicago: American Library Association, 1940. 54 p. (For an annotation see page 143.)

ROSENBERG, RALPH P.
Bibliographies of Theses in America. (In the BULLETIN OF BIBLIOGRAPHY for September–December, 1945, and January–April, 1946.)

Constitutes a supplement to GUIDE TO BIBLIOGRAPHIES (Palfrey and Coleman), with corrections and additions.

WOODRESS, JAMES L.
Doctoral Dissertations in American Literature 1891–1955. Durham, North Carolina: Duke University Press, 1957. 100 p.

Comprises 2,500 theses written at approximately one hundred universities in the United States and Western Europe. Includes completed theses and those in progress. The arrangement is alphabetical according to author and according to topic.

". . . the whole is carefully prepared and, of course, offers a most valuable tool to all advanced students and researchers in the field of American literature"–(AMERICAN LITERATURE, XXIX, November, 1957, 343).

Index to Authors

Index to Titles

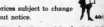